A JOURNEY WITH GOD

MEETING GOD IN MISSIONS

JIM
McDONALD

Contents

Foreword

Introduction

Chapter One   The Journey Begins 9

Chapter Two   Building Momentum 19

Chapter Three   Following God into the Dominican Republic 27

Chapter Four   A Place to Call Home 41

Chapter Five   Following God into Haiti 51

Chapter Six   Leaders And Leadings..65

Chapter Seven   Following God into La Vega 79

Chapter Eight   A Blessed Partnership..91

Chapter Nine   God's Purpose 109

Conclusion

*With thanks to Pamela Mayle,
Sandy Mayle, and Gil Jacobs
for their assistance in writing this book,
and to Mary Lou,
my wife of fifty-one years*

FOREWORD

When I first met Jim McDonald in 1992 he was the Athletic Director at Edinboro University. I had no idea how God was going to use Jim to present opportunities for myself and others to experience God through Meeting God in Missions (MGM). Following the path presented by Henry Blackaby and Claude King in their book *Experiencing God: Knowing and Doing the Will of God,* Jim has modeled the way to experiencing God by obeying Him and joining Him where He is working. Through MGM, Jim has provided opportunities for people throughout the United States to go on short-term missions trips and meet God in a unique way as they join Him in serving the people on the island of Hispaniola.

Meeting God in Missions was formed in 2001 as a nondenominational, not-for-profit ministry seeking to support the body of Christ through short-term missions ventures. I was privileged to help Jim McDonald obtain MGM's non-profit designation, and then to watch their amazing growth into a full-fledged ministry. As of December, 2008, MGM had conducted over 125 short-term missionary trips to the Dominican Republic and Haiti. These trips included construction teams, Bible school teams, baseball clinics, medical teams, optical teams, village care teams, and evangelism teams.

Contributions, gifts, and grants increased from $283,480 in 2001 to $626,864 in 2008, and 99% of MGM's expenditures go toward programs. The ministry has no employees and pays no compensation. An MGM trip costs approximately $1000, and many participants have returned multiple times, which indicates a high level of motivation on their part. For more information, please go to their website at *www.meetinggodinmissions.com*

As one of my doctoral research projects I did a case study of Jim's leadership of Meeting God in Missions and found him to be a servant-leader who sincerely tries to follow the example of Jesus Christ. Jim focuses his leadership efforts on providing MGM participants (a) air travel, (b) safe and clean housing, (c) nourishing meals, (d) worship services, (e) opportunities for service, (f) translators, and (g) spiritually inspiring devotions. Inspiration for the ministry comes from the scripture in 1 John 3:17: "If anyone has material possessions and sees his brother in need but has no pity on him, how can the love of God be in him?" (NIV).

With this background information in mind, I hope you will enjoy reading the MGM story from its earliest beginnings to the present day as told by Jim McDonald. I believe you will find in these pages an amazing story about people who are experiencing God as they join Him where He is working on the island of Hispaniola.

Gilbert A. Jacobs, PhD, Erie, PA

If anyone has material possessions
and sees his brother in need
but has no pity on him,
how can the love of God be in him?

- 1 John 3:17 NIV

INTRODUCTION

Big Russ and Jim

This is a story about a boy born in West Virginia in 1938. His childhood was very difficult and he used those struggles to reach for success in high school, college, and professional athletics (two-time college basketball All-American, leading national scorer - 1960, drafted into the NBA, tried out for the Olympics - 1960, NAIA Coach of the Year - 1974, led the USA team to a gold medal in Israel.)

At the age of 12, he accepted Jesus Christ as his Savior, but he had a difficult time living the Christian life. Although he was successful in sports and the accumulation of wealth, he had an empty spot in his heart that he couldn't fill. By 1989, he was faced with divorce and losing everything he loved. Finally, he came to a personal crisis and made a monumental decision to turn his life over to God and join Him on an amazing journey.

As you read this book, I pray that God will touch your heart and show you how he can use you on your journey here on earth. His faithfulness, His grace, His love, and His strength is available to all who are obedient to Him. Over the last twenty--plus years, God has changed me from who I was into someone He wanted me to be. He has provided the resources and people, and opened all the doors for the work he has called me to do. I pray as you read this, it will touch your heart and you will allow Him to change you into who He wants you to be, and you will be a blessing to others.

May God bless you,
Jim McDonald

1

THE JOURNEY BEGINS

My name is Jim McDonald. Today I am a believer in Jesus Christ and leader of Meeting God in Missions, an organization that conducts multiple yearly trips to the Dominican Republic, ministering to Dominicans and Haitians there. I want to tell you about the journey God has been taking me on, a journey that began long before I became a Christian.

Clearly, as I look back over my life, the conditions and events of my childhood prepared me for ministry in the Dominican Republic and Haiti, where the people are so poor and in need. In fact, my first mission trip was a flashback to my early years in West Virginia.

Times were difficult in those days. It was in the forties, a time when many people in our area of West Virginia were struggling, sometimes going without food or even going to their neighbors to ask for food. We were in that group. One of the most humiliating experiences of my childhood was knocking on doors in Bridgeport, West Virginia, to ask if we could have a sandwich. To this day I cannot get those memories out of my mind. I saw the same thing when I visited the Dominican Republic and Haiti. People had nothing, and even if they weren't asking for help, it was obvious they were in need.

My childhood was not a very pleasant one for other reasons, too. My father was a big man at six-foot-two, two hundred and sixty pounds. He was very abusive, with a horrible drinking habit and a violent temper. His rage caused a lot of confusion, pain and suffering in our home on many occasions.

My family moved around quite a bit when I was young. By the time I was ten years old, we had lived in six different houses. That same year, my father left and my mother, my older brother, Russell, age thirteen, and I found ourselves on our own. Russell and I continued to attend school, but because we had little money we were not well-clothed or well-fed. The only time I recall seeing a doctor was when my finger was nearly cut off in a mixer and I had to have it sewn back on. I don't believe I saw another doctor until I got to college. We just couldn't afford it.

During my youth, a lot of anger and resentment built up inside me because of our circumstances and the way people looked at us. Over time I became fairly proficient in playing sports and I took a lot of my anger out on my competitors, trying to get even for the things I didn't have in life.

When I was thirteen years old, my brother left to play professional baseball with the St. Louis Browns, now the Baltimore Orioles. That was an adjustment, because my brother was a good athlete and I'd looked up to him. Now, it was just my mother and me. As time went on, though, I grew taller and stronger and my athletic skills improved. I had the opportunity to play football, basketball and baseball in high school and was eventually awarded a scholarship that paid my way to West Virginia Wesleyan College.

Without that scholarship, I would have never been able to leave Bridgeport, because we didn't own a car and we couldn't afford to ride the bus; we either walked or thumbed. In fact, the college had to come and pick me up that next fall.

Yet as I look back on my childhood, God was involved in it all from the very beginning. He gave me the ability to play sports, then used that ability to get me to college and prepare me for work among the Dominicans and Haitians.

Redirections

My journey beyond high school, however, had many twists and turns in the road. It seemed that every time something was set to happen in my life, an event would suddenly occur that completely changed my direction.

I was a good student in high school and I went to college with plans to study pre-med and become a doctor. A physician in my hometown liked sports and decided that if I finished my studies at West Virginia Wesleyan, he would pay my way through medical school. So, funded by my athletic scholarship, I worked hard in college and got good grades while playing basketball and baseball.

The first day of my junior year, the physician from Bridgeport dropped over dead. There I was, starting my junior year in college with many math and chemistry courses completed, but no way to get to med school. I decided to continue with math and chemistry anyway, and got my teaching degree instead.

Meanwhile, I was excelling in basketball and baseball. As a result, I was drafted into the National Basketball Association to play for the Cincinnati Royals, now the Sacramento Kings organization. Soon I was headed for their training camp with a contract offer. It didn't promise a large amount of money, but then nobody was making big money back in those days.

The night before I was to leave for training camp, my appendix suddenly ruptured. I ended up in the hospital for several days, lost a lot of weight, and missed training camp. Before I could get back into any kind of condition to join them, they had started the season and my opportunity to play in the NBA that year was terminated.

I taught for awhile, thought I had an opportunity to play again, and once more encountered a problem that prevented it. I wasn't walking closely with God and I didn't understand what He was doing; I only knew that every time I closed in on a goal, something came up to keep me from reaching it.

Then in 1962 I had an opportunity to coach basketball at Edinboro University. To my surprise, no accident or emergency operation kept me from taking the position of head basketball coach at Edinboro. I stayed there until 1993. Over that thirty-two year span, I was first the head basketball coach and eventually the Director of Athletics, overseeing Edinboro U's sports program..

Running that athletic program was excellent preparation for running mission trips to Haiti and the Dominican Republic. I had to arrange plane flights to take athletic teams, marching bands, cheerleaders, and university personnel from one place to another. I did this for so many years it became natural for me to lead people and to move them from one section of the country to another without much problem.

When I was invited to go on my first mission trip, I didn't yet understand that all through my life God had been preparing me for just such a thing. He'd been developing not only my abilities but also my understanding. Because of my childhood, I understood what poverty was. I understood what it was like to be mistreated. I understood how it felt to have people look down on you, thinking you were not in their class. I'd learned, during my last two years in high school and throughout my college summers, what it meant to work hard. Employed by a carbon factory, I'd worked in blast furnaces twenty feet below the ground, where the temperature sometimes topped one hundred degrees even on my midnight shift. I'd certainly looked forward to the day I could say goodbye to the furnaces of United Carbon Company and get a life that would be a whole lot easier.

So when I went down and saw the people in the Dominican Republic and Haiti, it took me back to the days when my mother and I struggled to survive. I understood something of what they were experiencing. And later, when I led my first mission trip, I'd assumed we were going to minister to the Dominicans in general. I was drawn, though, to the poorest of them - until I went into the sugar cane fields. There, in the villages of Haitian families who'd come to harvest the Dominican sugar cane, were the most needy, the most looked-down-on, the truly outcast. It became very apparent to me that my heart was with these Haitians.

So through the years I have found great joy and peace in taking teams to many of the DR's Haitian villages to provide food, clothing, finances, eye glasses, dental care, medical treatment, Vacation Bible School, sports equipment and all kinds of health benefits in an attempt to make life a little more tolerable for these people.

Many of them have been in the sugar cane fields all their lives. They have never had the opportunity to travel a paved road. Many had never seen a dentist until we came, and most of the villagers had never seen a doctor before my son showed up a few years ago. It has been a rewarding experience just to meet these Haitians and then witness the improvement in their health and the change in their lives. My faith has grown as I've realized how God used my days in West Virginia to develop in me this love for them.

God has been faithful to transform lives in those sugar cane fields – and not just Haitians, but also the Americans who've come on the mission trips. Some who visit the Haitian villages spend the entire time sitting and crying, unable to believe that that human beings could be treated as these people are. The children, sometimes starving, sick, and naked, especially touch their heart.

What happens to those Americans isn't a head change; it is a heart change. And it has become very evident to me, as I've studied and matured over the last fifteen years, that God is more interested in changing our heart than our head. He has chosen to use the sugar cane fields for that purpose. Probably the heart that He has changed the most has been mine, because after I came back from that first twelve-day trip, my life has never been the same. I have certainly made a lot of mistakes, but God has been faithful, and for His work in my heart I am eternally grateful.

But I am ahead of my story…

Meeting God

By 1992 I was the Athletic Director at Edinboro University and things were looking good – on the outside.

I had been successful in everything I'd ever tried as a young athlete. I'd gone on to make money and acquire many material possessions. My wife, our sixteen-year-old son, and I lived in a beautiful home (two older sons had moved on to their own families and successful careers). Yet there was something missing and I didn't know what to do about it. I had a hole in my heart that I couldn't fill with possessions, money or success, and I was failing miserably in my marriage and in my relationship with my sons.

God had already been working behind the scenes to draw me to Himself, to change my life, and to make me someone He could use. Through all my searching and struggling, He was there - but I hadn't yet recognized Him.

At eight o'clock one Friday evening, I began flipping through television channels, looking for a basketball game. In the process, I dropped my remote on the floor, and when I picked it up and tried to change the channel, nothing happened. I looked up to see the introduction to In Touch Ministries. As I continued to unsuccessfully click the remote, the speaker assured me, "God meets your needs." I said to myself, Well, God never meets my needs and I don't know why somebody else thinks He would meet theirs.

My youngest son, Matt, observed all this from the couch and finally suggested, "Why don't we watch this tonight?" As a favor to him, we watched that segment of Charles Stanley's series, God Meets Yours Needs. At the conclusion, Matt suggested we watch the program again the following week and invite some of his friends to see it also.

So the next Friday evening, three of his friends joined us.

I would look back on that night as one of the defining moments in my life. While Stanley spoke, my son and his friends sat and talked about God (Matt doing most of the talking). The program ended at nine o'clock and at midnight, after listening to them for three more hours, I went to bed. The next morning I learned that Matt had led one of his friends in a prayer to receive Christ as his Savior. (Eleven years later, that friend became the first president of the university that MGM built outside of Cape Haitian, Haiti. God's hand was in this from the very beginning).

The Covenant

Shortly after the *God Meets Your Needs* series ended, I went into my bedroom and knelt down and, for two or three hours, tearfully begged God to help me. I knew very little about God, the Holy Spirit, or the Bible, yet as I cried out to God I remember using the word "covenant." I made a covenant that night with God: if he would reunite my family, I would go anywhere and do anything that he asked me to do until the day I died. I really didn't understand what I was saying, but when I arose from my knees, I realized that I was different. I felt like a weight had been lifted off my back.

Three days later, around 9:30 am, I received a call at my office unlike any I'd ever received before. Would I consider working on a part-time basis for a Christian organization? I agreed to think about it (I'm not sure I understood enough to say, "I'll pray about it").

Shortly after 10:00 I got a second phone call, asking if I would consider serving another Christian organization. It seemed rather humorous to receive two phone calls of this nature within an hour, but I was forgetting the covenant I'd made with God.

Just before noon I got a third call, this one from Rick Crocker, pastor of First Alliance Church in nearby Erie, where I now attended. Would there be any way that I could help them as church administrator? I hung up the phone... and then it dawned on me. I had made a covenant with God, a promise that I was determined to keep, and I had forgotten about it.

That afternoon I walked into the President's office of Edinboro University and, after thirty-two years there, handed him a letter of resignation. I was starting a journey without knowing where I was going, how I was going to get there, or what was going to happen. But I knew that there had to be a change in my life.

After handing in my resignation, I called my pastor about the church administrator's job, and started on this journey with God.

The Transformation

I was now passionately studying the Bible. Although I had attended church most of my life, I don't believe I had read a chapter in the Bible in over forty years. I knew only two Scripture verses: "Jesus wept," and John 3:16. Yet now I was captivated by what I was reading. The first day, I read perhaps eight or nine hours. One month later, I was reading the Bible sixteen to eighteen hours a day, even awakening in the night and turning on the light to write down thoughts I might forget by morning.

Mary Lou moved out of the bedroom because she couldn't sleep. After filling up several legal pads, I confessed my fears to her. Was I having mental problems? What was going on? Yet after I finished reading the New Testament and writing down what God was teaching me, I was in awe of how much I could remember.

For the next five and a half years we continued our Friday nights with Charles Stanley. What started as three friends grew to twenty-five by the sixth night, and eventually to around one hundred kids. They came from Pittsburgh, Cleveland, and even Canada to attend what they now dubbed "Friday Night Alive."

The meetings started at 7:00 p.m., and we finally had to set a 1:00 a.m. time limit. To see one hundred kids worship for five or six hours on a Friday night was absolutely phenomenal. During that time, we continued to videotape Charles Stanley's program. Each Friday night we would show the tape and then break up into groups for prayer. Afterward we'd come back together for worship and testimonies. It was a great time of fellowship. We had healing services, concerts with professional singers, and times of worship led by a talented Dominican worship leader. We would pray for something and God would answer those prayers. It was amazing what was transpiring.

And although I didn't see it at the time, lives were being changed. Many young people were saved, and from this group came missionaries, youth pastors, and worship leaders. Probably the person who grew the most was me. God was changing my life right in front of me, although I didn't yet see it. I became passionate about reading not only the Bible, but also books on the Holy Spirit, Whom I'd never heard of in all my years of sitting in the church.

As I grew to understand who the Holy Spirit was and what He wanted to do in my life and the empowerment He would bring to accomplish it all, God transformed me. In the process, He saved my marriage. My wife, my sons, and I began to grow closer together. I owe it all to God.

The Adventure

By 1994, I had become the church administrator at First Alliance Church. Pastor Rick had gotten involved with an organization called Adventures in Mission, which was planning a trip to the town of Hato Mayor in the Dominican Republic. He and my wife each decided they were going on that mission trip and I was going to go, too. I, however, had little interest in missions beyond our local City Mission and I was equally determined that I was not going.

That didn't stop them. Mary Lou insisted I get a passport. To please her, I went and got a passport but I told her I didn't think I was going to go to the Dominican Republic. We discussed the twelve-day trip for months, right up to the day we were supposed to leave. Even then I tried to say I couldn't find my passport, but she knew exactly where it was so I had no way out.

Eight people from our church loaded into two vehicles and headed for the Cleveland airport. When we arrived, the first van emptied and headed back to Erie. Soon afterward, we discovered that my carry-on and passport had been left in it (surely it was divine intervention, I thought). I expected to get into the second vehicle and return to Erie, certain now that God was letting me off the hook and I wouldn't have to go to the Dominican Republic. But Rick Crocker got into the remaining van, drove about a third of the way back to Erie, overtook the first vehicle, got my carry-on and passport, and returned to the Cleveland airport in time for me to get on the airplane.

So away we went to build a church for the Dominicans.

When I got to Hato Mayor, I couldn't believe how much it looked like my hometown of Bridgeport, West Virginia, in my growing-up years. There were no paved streets, nearly everyone was dirt poor, most if not all the kids were barefoot, and the younger ones didn't wear clothes. They were filthy, and they drank the same filthy water that we got out of the river to mix into mortar.

It was heartbreaking. Every time I saw one of those children, I saw myself forty years ago - a kid knocking on people's doors, asking for food. In fact, the first night in Hato Mayor I didn't know if I could make it until daylight. But twelve days later, I didn't want to leave. God had done a work in my life in those twelve days that I would never forget. I believe every single person who went on that trip felt the same way. It was a cultural shock that penetrated our hearts, not just our heads. The need was unbelievable, and the experience was life-changing.

The following year we returned to Hato Mayor to complete the church we had started. This time, I stayed in a different facility, an orphanage. We had a wonderful time and made some great friendships with the children, aged nine to twelve. I built them a little basketball hoop out in the dirt and tried to show them how to play basketball.

We worked hard and finished the church, and I thought my connection with the Dominican Republic was also finished. I had honored my pastor and pleased him and my wife and made two trips which had profoundly impacted my life.

On the last night, it was time to celebrate and go home. We went to the only place in town where we felt it was safe to eat - the ice cream parlor. While we are standing in line for ice cream, one of the members of our group announced that after we got our ice cream, we needed to follow him. He wanted to show us something we wouldn't believe.

We walked back behind the ice cream parlor and discovered a

woman named Pastor Ondina Barriola. She was preaching in the grease pit of a big three-bay truck garage. Her congregation of about one hundred people listened from white lawn chairs set up in a gravel driveway. That was her church.

Pastor Ondina was blind, had no fingers and only one leg, and preached from her wheelchair. As divine

Jim and Pastor Ondina

intervention would have it, the only English teacher in town, a young man by the name of Henry Mercedes, was a member of her congregation. As we stood at the edge of the crowd, watching and listening, Henry got up and put his arm around her, interrupting her preaching. We watched as he said something to her.

She whispered something back to him, after which he turned to us and asked, "Are you the ones?"

Rick Crocker asked, "What do you mean by 'Are you the ones'?"

Henry proceeded to tell us that Pastor Ondina (now seventy-one) had contracted leprosy when she was twenty years old. The doctors told her to go home and die because there was no cure and no hope for her. She went home and made a covenant with God that if he would heal her, she would serve him the rest of her life. For fifty-one years she preached and waited, holding on to God's promise that before she died someone would come and build her a church if she was faithful. Now she wanted to know if we were the ones.

No, Rick replied, we were not the ones; we had come to build an Alliance Church in Hato Mayor. We were going home the next day and this was probably our last mission trip to Hato Mayor.

We did return home the next day. But that night, I went to bed and lay sleepless. All I could see was the woman in the wheelchair. In fact, this happened for perhaps two months. One day at church I told the pastor, "Rick, I have to go back and build this woman a church." (I didn't really recognize it as God's plan; I thought it was mine.) I said, "I can't sleep. Every time I go to bed I see this woman. This is something I've got to do. I am going to lead a trip down there."

I did take a team to the DR in 1995 and we built Pastor Ondina a church. God had prepared me, I would later realize, for such a venture. I knew how to lead a trip. I knew how do to much of what would be required. What I didn't know was… He was preparing a lot of other people, too, and we were all part of a much greater plan.

In hindsight, it is easy to see the birth of MGM as a wonderful work and gift of God. However, living through the days and years of knitting it all together were difficult and often painful.

Our marriage was indeed in big trouble. Jim's struggles are chronicled in these pages; mine were mostly concerted efforts to build a hard shell, maintain distance, and try to save our family from becoming a statistic (and I still marvel that I was the one who insisted we try a mission trip - I really was not an eager flyer!).

Again, what was obscured in day-to-day living has become clear, God at work! Although Jim and I are still weaving the unfinished tapestry, we are now working toward the same end and praising God for His grace and love.

- Mary Lou McDonald

I vividly remember my first visit to the Dominican Republic. My father and I were stationed in an orphanage run by a pastor and his wife. Every day the caregivers cooked, cleaned, and watched over the little boys living there. With a bit of broken Spanish, I got to know each of them by name. One boy dreamt of becoming a doctor, another a professional baseball player. A number of them were brothers, and some had heart breaking stories.

There were only a few of us on the trip, and the boys took quite a liking to us. They called me "Mateo," and loved to play basketball with me. I remember talking to them about God, and who I knew Him to be. Most said they knew Him as well. We shared stories about our life experiences. I know part of their fascination with me was because they had never had much, if any, contact with an American. But that intrigue provided a fertile ground for meaningful friendships to grow.

At the end of the week, it was time to say goodbye to those boys. My heart broke. I knew I was leaving to go back to a place of lavish luxury. A place so different from the lives these little boys knew. We all hugged and shed some tears as I left for home. But rather than just feeling compassion for the hardships they faced, I felt so blessed to have had the opportunity to know them.

Their world seemed like such a stark contrast to mine. Their lives weren't hindered by the busy schedules, deadlines, and material things that had been so consuming to me. All they had was each other. All they had was relationship. And it reminded me of the simplicity and value of relationship. We serve a relational God. We find meaning, growth, and healing in our relationship with Him and others. Jesus said the two greatest commands are to love God with all your heart, soul, mind, and strength; and to love your neighbor as yourself. Interesting that both of those charges are calls to be in loving relationships. I think I found that in my first trip to the Dominican. I found it in a bunch of little boys who had an unhindered joy in getting to know me, and I them.

- Matt McDonald, Psy. D.

BUILDING MOMENTUM

Around this time I was asked by an elder in our church to consider becoming the president of the Edinboro Conference Campground, our area Christian & Missionary Alliance church camp. I assured him that I had no interest of being the president of the camp; in fact, I hadn't even realized there was such a place even though I lived in Edinboro.

A week later the elder told me he had nominated me as president, to which I replied, "Well, I tell you, I'm not really interested." We discussed it further, and I came away confident I wouldn't have to worry about the nomination. They surely wouldn't elect a president who had never seen the campground and hardly knew anyone connected with the place.

The following Saturday the Conference committee unanimously elected the sole nominee – me – as president, and I went for my first look at Edinboro Conference Campground.

A Dismal Situation

While I was assessing the facilities, an older gentleman approached and introduced himself as Mr. Loomis, the caretaker. He showed me around, eventually leading me to an old farmhouse, the ground floor of which served as the cafeteria and the upstairs as the speaker's lodging. The wood-frame house was probably seventy to eighty years old. The foundation was deteriorating and the kitchen floor sloped badly. In fact, the health board had condemned the kitchen and given the camp one year to repair or replace it.

As a young Christian I didn't know much about how God works, I just knew it was a dismal situation. I asked Mr. Loomis about money in the budget to redo the kitchen and repair the foundation, and learned that finances were tight. The camp was just barely meeting the bills; there was no money for such a project.

If we were to rebuild, there was an open space in the center of the grounds that had potential. But we had no money, and I had little construction experience beyond that brief introduction in the Dominican Republic.

A Foundation Is Laid

Nevertheless, I went back to church and started asking around about builders. I discovered that one of the biggest builders in Erie attended our church. Herb Logan had built hundreds of homes over the years. So I went out to lunch with him, where I further learned that his block layers, Charlie Young and Sons, were Christians.

I called Charlie's son, Terry, who was helping to oversee the block laying under Herb Logan, and asked if I could meet with him. I told Terry about the presidency I had received by default, my inexperience, and the financial troubles of the camp. Would he come over and give me some advice and maybe some help?

I believe he took pity on my ignorance. We met at Edinboro Camp and looked at the facility. He proceeded to tell me that we needed to have footers dug out, we needed concrete, we needed block, and so on. Every time he added something I could see we also needed more and more money.

Finally I asked, "Do you think there are any Christians out there who would be willing to help us?" He didn't know very many believers in the construction business, but thought that he might be able to talk his block company into donating a few block.

A week or two later, Terry called with good news. They had constructed a huge grocery store in Erie using beautiful split-faced block, and there were many left over from the project. Terry had convinced the block company to donate them as a tax deduction for the camp. The next thing I knew, truckload after truckload of split-faced block were being delivered to the campgrounds.

I began to draw up plans for a kitchen and dining room facility. As the plans progressed, it seemed wise to add two conference rooms. This, however, put the building out of kilter, so we added two large bunk rooms and bathrooms. With the furnace room, air conditioning and a storage room for food, we were now looking at a large facility approximately 80-by-60-feet.

Terry and his family agreed to lay the block, but they needed cement for the footers. Terry suggested a cement plant just three miles down the road, so I visited the place and met a man who knew me from attending basketball games I'd coached. He related our situation to the owner, who agreed to donate and deliver all the cement for the footers and the floor.

Now we had the blocks and the concrete; all we had to do was dig the footer. This was my first experience with footers, but I rounded up some men with shovels and picks and we started digging, with Terry coming by periodically to give instructions.

So when the footers were ready to pour, in came the concrete trucks as promised, at no cost to us, from an owner I'd never personally met. Nearby, ready and waiting, lay blocks donated by a company representative I had never met. And once those blocks were laid and the walls were up, three cement finishers who had heard what we were doing volunteered to smooth out the floors. Later, a plumber came from Warren, Pennsylvania, to help put the plumbing in the floor. It was amazing, although I was still too immature a Christian to see God's hand in it all.

The Workers Gather

Eventually it was time to put a roof on the huge facility. I returned to Herb Logan and asked if he knew anybody who did roofs. He could see, as we talked, that I was completely out of my league. He finally agreed to contact the company that made his trusses and see what he could do.

A couple of weeks later Herb called me. The company had already been out to the campgrounds to measure the building, and now were preparing to design the trusses. Herb would see that we got the trusses, sheeting and shingles at no cost. I don't know whether he paid for it or it was donated, but suddenly we had designs and materials, including a crane to install the trusses, fully funded.

Herb instructed me to recruit people to help install the trusses and lay the sheeting and shingles. I began to talk to pastors of the churches connected with the camp, and soon many of those churches jumped on board. Some hadn't been very involved in the campgrounds previously, but they understood the desperate need for a new dining facility and welcomed the opportunity to get behind the building project.

We announced two Saturday work days. About forty workers, people I'd never met, came from these churches. None of us knew that on those two Saturdays friendships would be formed and skills demonstrated that would prove useful on a far larger scale. I had no clue that the majority of those forty workers would end up going on mission trips with me. God, however, was setting the stage for those trips and he was using our dining facility, Loomis Lodge (named after the faithful old caretaker), to bring all these people together.

After two Saturdays, the shingles were on and we still had probably less than three thousand dollars invested in this project, from the footer to the roof. My awe grew - although I still hadn't fully figured God into the mix yet.

A plumbing company from Erie donated all the shower and

plumbing fixtures, and our plumbers and friends installed them. Electricity came next... and now I was worried. I'd called various people, but no one was willing to help. Then one evening, as I was sweeping the Loomis Lodge floor, a vehicle pulled into the camp and a man approached me.

"I've been watching this thing being constructed and just wondered what is going on."

I told him the story, as I told anybody that would listen, and added, "I'm at a point now where I'm kind of lost because I don't know any electricians and we need lights. I've been calling electricians but I can't get anybody interested. By the way, what do you do?"

He said he was an electrician. If I wanted to meet him tomorrow night at five o'clock, he said, he could give me four hours. He and I started the next night, and the following night he brought another worker. He and his friend, with me as the "grunt," got the electric work done within approximately six weeks. It was then that I began to see God's hand in all of this.

An Answer to Prayer

We now had a beautiful facility... but no beds, no tables, no chairs, no kitchen equipment. One morning while I was cleaning up around the construction site, Mr. Loomis walked in. I shared my burden with him: we still needed perhaps forty to fifty thousand dollars to furnish the building.

"Well, let's sit right down here and pray about it," Mr. Loomis responded, so we did.

Around four o'clock in the afternoon, Mr. Loomis returned. "Remember that prayer we had this morning?"

"Yes."

"Well, I was down front mowing when a guy pulled over to the side of the road and told me that he worked for a lumber mill and had always admired the timber on our campground. He said he'd checked out the timber and wanted to know if we were interested in selling it." The camp owned about thirty-five wooded acres.

" I told him," continued Mr. Loomis, "that we had done just that a few years ago and we got five thousand dollars for it and there was such an uproar from the people who attended the camp, I never wanted to get involved in that again."

I agreed. "We need forty to fifty thousand dollars and we'd make enemies - and I've only been connected with this group for less than a year. For five thousand, I don't think it's worth it."

"Well, the guy told me he thought he could get twenty thousand for us."

Twenty thousand.

I said, "Did you get his phone number?"

He had, so I went home and called the man. He'd already been walking around the campground looking at the trees that day, and he was willing to come the next day and mark all the trees that were eighteen inches in diameter. Then he would give us a firm bid.

After our conversation, I called every company in the area that bought timber. I told them I had approximately thirty-five acres of timber that were ready to be cut, and I needed to have the bids within two weeks, when the matter of furnishing the facility would come to the monthly board meeting.

The next day I received a twenty-thousand dollar bid from the man who had stopped and talk to Mr. Loomis. And almost every day, for the next twelve days, we received another bid in the mail.

The bids went exactly like this: the second bid was twenty-five thousand, and the third bid was thirty (these people seemed to know everyone was bidding because each bid increased by five thousand dollars). The next bids were thirty-five, forty, and on to forty-five thousand. Three days before Saturday's meeting, we got what I assumed was the final bid of fifty thousand dollars. I was stunned. God was truly at work. With the fifty thousand dollars we would be able to pay for the tables, chairs, beds, and kitchen, as well as for a heating and air conditioning unit for the facility. We were elated.

Friday evening the phone rang. Yet another man wanted to bid on our timber. "I'm sorry, it's too late," I told him. "We're opening the bids tomorrow at ten o'clock."

He said, "If I hand you a bid before tomorrow morning at ten, will you accept it?"

"If I have the bid before I walk into the conference room at ten, we will accept your bid because that is what we told everyone we would do."

His bid, the last one, was for $54,500, and that's what we sold the timber for. Interestingly, that was the only bid that was not in five thousand dollar increments! The total remaining cost for the facility was paid for in answer to a prayer that Mr. Loomis had suggested we offer that morning at the campground.

God's Plan Unfolds...

Now we had the money to purchase everything needed to complete the facility, we'd spent only a few thousand dollars, and God had provided it all, including the workers.

God had called me to be president of Edinboro Camp, although I hadn't wanted the job. He'd allowed the old kitchen to be condemned, according to His plan. That plan then brought together generous companies and willing builders and block layers and electricians and plumbers and cooks... for something more than Loomis Lodge and Edinboro Campgrounds. God was laying the groundwork for what would soon become Meeting God in Missions.

Loomis Lodge, Edinboro, PA

... And Expands

Shortly before I was appointed campground president, I took on another unlikely role. Jim Heibel, an associate pastor at First Alliance, was moving on to a church in New York. He'd been an excellent teacher and I had attended his large Sunday School class.

At that time I was serving as church administrator, and Pastor Rick decided that I should teach the class until a new associate came and took it over. I wasn't sure how my background as a basketball coach qualified me to teach a Sunday School class and I was very apprehensive, but I didn't want to disappoint him. Besides, he assured me it would only be for a short period of time.

I agreed to teach the class just until someone came to take it over. I gathered all the notes that I had written a few years before, with the books I had read on the Holy Spirit, and prepared to teach the Sunday School class.

That was fifteen years ago. I have used those notes and books over the years as I teach the class the things God showed me when I had an experience with Him – about the need in my heart, my entering into a covenant with God, and my journey into a life-changing encounter with the Holy Spirit.

Little did I know that block-layer Terry Young would begin attending our church and my Sunday School class, and become not only a great friend, but the leader of the construction company for Meeting God in Missions which now probably includes over two hundred people. Terry was the individual God would use to bring block layers, carpenters and laborers into this mission work, and he would influence many lives and bring many people to the kingdom.

Now, looking back, I'm awed by how God has worked in all of this.

It's amazing to see how God used the Edinboro project to forge a friendship and a great working relationship between Jim and myself, and to see where He has led us...

I went on my first missions trip in 1998. Our purpose was to repair damage caused when Hurricane George came through the DR. I went with eleven other guys, including my dad, Charlie, and my thirteen-year-old son, Adam (it was during buck hunting season, which I'd never missed since I was twelve years old!). We stayed at the orphanage, and had our first experience with Jim McDonald's morning devotions. My dad said Jim was the best preacher he ever listened to because he could understand him.

Dad was afraid of the DR people at first, thinking he would not return home alive! Nothing could have been farther from the truth – that trip proved to be one of our most memorable experiences. We loved the friendly Dominicans, and the people in the Haitian village won our hearts. My dad especially loved the children.

During that first trip we built two churches. Also, while Adam and I laid the block on Charlie Atlas' church, my dad built the famous outhouse with our names inscribed on the front: "Charlie, Terry, Adam."

That trip created a burning desire in my heart to return to build more churches, schools, and pastor's homes, and to invite other construction workers like myself to experience meeting God in the mission field. In fact, I now desire to start each year off by going on a mission trip. A year without going to the DR or Haiti would be empty.

The MGM trips eventually opened my eyes to see that the work we were doing was not about laying the block but it was about people's needs; they were more important than the actual job. Likewise, when I returned home I found myself more focused on people and their hurts and better able to talk to fellow workers about their heart and soul instead of discussing the next job.

When I'm back home in the work world, I share the experience I had on the mission field. If that person shows interest in what I'm saying, I feel God leads me to follow up and get a commitment from them to go on a mission trip. I've discovered that men like myself need to get away from the everyday pressures of life to concentrate on what God is doing around them and then find a relationship with Him. Many have found Christ as their personal Savior and their lives have been impacted forever, as mine has been.

Over the last twelve years, Jim McDonald has set a good example for me. He has inspired me to be a better Christian and to be bolder in witnessing. We've enjoyed great camaraderie over those eighteen trips, and experienced many adventures while working at unusual jobsites. We often started jobs at the outset that we believed could never be completed by the end of the week... but we usually finished early! And Jim's lessons were with us through it all: "Stay flexible!" and "It's not about the block!"

- Terry Young
Erie, Pa

3

FOLLOWING GOD INTO THE DOMINICAN REPUBLIC

In 1998 there was a hurricane in the Dominican Republic that destroyed a number of Christian Missionary & Alliance churches located out in the sugar cane fields. At that time, the U.S. president of the C&MA Men's Ministry was a man by the name of Fred Jennings from Akron, Ohio.

Fred called one day and asked if I would be willing to help the Alliance by going to the Dominican Republic for an extended time. My job would be to oversee groups of men who would come on one-week trips, Saturday to Saturday, to rebuild the Alliance churches that had been destroyed. He would supply the men and the money for the facilities; I, in turn, would meet the men at the airport and oversee the rebuilding of the churches.

I told him that the first week I would take our building crew, headed up by Terry Young, to start the construction process, and then I would stay on until all the facilities were completed. So Terry, with his father Charlie and son Adam – three generations - joined me on a mission trip to the Dominican Republic to start the project.

As we prepared for the trips, it became apparent that we were going to need someone in the Dominican Republic to purchase supplies and to coordinate details from that end. God kept bringing Henry Mercedes back to my mind. He was the young man we'd met at Pastor Ondina's church behind the ice cream parlor, on the last night of my second trip.

I contacted Henry and asked him if he would help us. He agreed, and became a great ally for us down there. He prepared all the sites and helped us get the materials we needed. He also stayed with us for an extended period of time as we went back and forth to the airports each

Saturday to pick up new people. Henry eventually took on the responsibility of coordinating trips and scheduling both worksites and churches to visit for evening worship. He helped us purchase land and deal with various situations that arose. God used him in a mighty way. Later on he became a pastor in Hato Mayor.

Haitian Village in the Dominican Republic

A Good Beginning

Overseeing the rebuilding of those C&MA churches proved to be quite an adventure. Fifteen to thirty men came each Saturday, stayed together at an orphanage, and worked for one week. They flew in from Washington state, Oregon, Minneapolis and all across the United States – a diverse group of men with a common interest in construction.

From day one we started our mornings at the worksites with prayer, in an effort to set a godly climate for the whole day and leave no doubt in anyone's mind that we were there to serve God.

Although I don't remember just how it came about, we also decided, when the first group arrived at the orphanage, to have a morning devotional time out on the basketball court. Everyone was awakened at daylight to gather outside. We read a chapter from the Bible, after which I made a few comments about the Scripture, challenged the men in their walk with God, and led in a prayer. Then we ate breakfast, climbed onto the backs of the trucks that transported us, and went out to work all day in the sugar cane fields. This routine continued for nine or ten weeks as teams came and went, building the churches.

That was the beginning of morning devotions for what later became the organization Meeting God in Missions. It was an outgrowth of what was happening in my own life. Since making my covenant with God, I had been immersing myself in the Bible. I was now also reading many other books in an effort to understand the Holy Spirit and my relationship with God. Yet I really didn't understand what was taking place; I didn't recognize the role of the Holy Spirit in my life. I had the desire, but I had neither the cognitive knowledge, nor the awareness, submission, or abiding necessary for an intimate relationship with God. I wanted to serve Him, but mostly in my own strength. My relationship with God was definitely from a distance.

As I studied the Old Testament, however, I was repeatedly reminded that in order to find God you had to seek him with all your heart. So I made a determination that I would start getting up at five o'clock every morning to seek God and to find out what he wanted to do in my life.

This decision changed my life. In fact, getting up at five o'clock in the morning has probably impacted me as much as anything I have ever done. I started to study the Bible rather than simply read it. My prayer life grew. My understanding of who I was also grew, and my relationship with God changed drastically.

The mission trips, too, began to change as we began sharing morning devotions together. I tried to pass on to the trip participants the many things God had been showing me. God eventually put it upon my heart, as I was preparing for my Sunday School class, to write a daily devotional booklet for the people who came on missions trips, so they could have something to follow along and take home to read. So I started getting up early in the morning and praying and listening to God all year long for material not only for teaching Sunday School each week, but also for morning devotionals that would be helpful to the people who came on the trips.

Writing a new seven-day devotional booklet each year has helped me grow in my walk with God as I more fully understand who He is and how the Holy Spirit empowers us. Our practice of morning devotions, started on that first trip, has been a blessing to many, many other people, too.

The Sugar Cane Villages

Just getting to the sugar cane fields was an adventure. Typically, we would ride in open-bed trucks for perhaps forty-five minutes, the last ten miles on a dirt path through sugar cane that rose higher than the vehicles. Finally we would come upon a village of Haitians – men, with their families, who had been hired by the Dominicans to harvest sugar cane. There were many, perhaps hundreds, of these villages in our area, with probably two to four hundred thousand Haitians working in huge sugar cane fields up to ten miles wide and forty miles long.

Eventually we heard the story behind these villages. Many of the people had walked over from Haiti (it was over three hundred miles just to the Haiti border). If they had come from Port-au-Prince, Haiti's capitol, they'd probably walked closer to five hundred miles. They came to the Dominican Republic to escape the severe poverty of their own country. Here they could make two dollars a day and have at least a little bit of food to eat.

Even so, it was a difficult, almost impossible life. Frequently, villages did not have water. To obtain water for drinking and cooking, they often had to walk five to seven miles one way, fill their containers, and return all those miles carrying their heavy burden, every day.

They had very little food. The men usually ate one meal every two days. One out of five children starved to death by the time they were four

years old. And they lived in deplorable conditions. Most families lived in one room, with a hole in the middle of the floor for a bathroom, which emptied outside into the sugar cane fields.

Our hearts were broken when we saw the conditions of these sugar cane villages and the people who lived in them. Although the Haitians were happy we were there, they had no hope for the future. It was a very humbling experience and God used the poverty to change many Americans' hearts and lives. As we

Haitian Sugar Cane Fields

spent nearly a week at each project site and became good friends with the villagers, we built relationships without knowing how God was going to use them. But now, years later, we see His hand in it all. For instead of working in Dominican towns, we now focus our ministry on the sugar cane villages that lie within about a forty-five mile radius of our headquarters in Hato Mayor.

New Doors Open

During our eight-to-ten-week stay at the orphanage, we attended Dominican church services in the evenings and observed these people as they worshipped God under a variety of conditions. Sometimes the people walked to the service; at other times they rode horses or donkeys. Some churches used oil lamps. Some had dirt floors. We even worshipped in churches made out of tree limbs and tin they had picked up along the road. It was an eye opener for us.

Needs and opportunities met us everywhere. Along with the obvious needs of the churches in which we worshipped, many people stopped at the orphanage where we stayed to inquire about the possibility of our group building them a church or putting a roof on an existing church or helping them in some other way. Henry passed along to us various requests that people brought to him. Consequently, at the conclusion of this adventure with God we got together and decided that we would go back again and build another church to be located in one of the poorest parts of town.

We went… and went again and again, in response to the needs and God's call. And as we began to make more and more trips to the Dominican Republic, more and more eyes were opened. When new people came along, their hearts were touched and they returned on subsequent trips, bringing friends with them. So we began to grow in numbers.

Soon, besides the construction workers, we started to bring Vacation Bible School teachers with us to teach the young kids. That was really a blessing because the workers could take a break and play with the kids during the day as well as working with laying blocks. It was an enjoyable experience for everybody.

The next year, 1999, interest had grown to the extent that we took two trips (soon we would be running multiple trips a year). For awhile we continued to stay at the orphanage, but eventually we were bringing forty to fifty people at a time and sleeping on the floor of the church as well as in the orphanage itself. We outgrew the facility, but not before making friends with the boys living there, two of whom eventually came to work for us and for the Lord.

For some, the trips became an annual event. The Youngs sometimes spent two or three weeks a year working in the DR. It made an impact on their lives and helped them grow in their Christian walk, and they came back excited and witnessing for Jesus. Their commitment and enthusiasm rubbed off onto everyone who went on the trips.

Another Ally

As we were getting our feet on the ground in Hato Mayor, God brought a lady across our path who became a great help to us. Ada Barriola

Lappot, like Henry Mercedes, attended Pastor Ondina's church. In fact, she was one of the leaders in that church, and a powerful Christian. She was also a lawyer, and as time went on she obtained an important job with the government in that part of the Dominican Republic and became a great help to us as we purchased land and built churches.

Later she would encourage us to start putting these properties in Meeting God in Mission's name so that we could gain credibility in the country as non-profit landowners. It took her five years, much hard work, and many trips to Santo Domingo, the country's capital, to obtain our non-profit status in the Dominican Republic. She never took a penny although she spent many, many hours working on our behalf. God blessed her for her faithfulness. In 2007 she became one of the judges in the country of the Dominican Republic, and she now works in Santo Domingo. God used her to help us, and I believe God worked through us to help her grow in her walk with Him.

Revival in Hato Mayor

In 1997, as I prayed about the upcoming trips, God began to talk to me about His plan for Hato Mayor. In fact, nearly every morning for over a year I had one recurring thought: I needed to meet with all the pastors in Hato Mayor and tell them that God was going to bring a revival to their town. I felt unworthy. How could I, a former basketball coach, not a preacher, have the audacity to inform over forty Dominican pastors that God was sending a revival to their area?

For many months I had a long conversation with God, telling him this was something I didn't want to do. Yet it continued to come to my mind, not only when I was praying but even while studying or just going about my day.

Aboard the airplane on one of our 1998 trips, as I was praying, I again sensed that I needed to meet with the pastors. I again told God that I didn't want to do it and I again felt God compelling me to do it. But since I could not envision ever having the opportunity to meet with them all in one place, I figured I was off the hook.

On our second evening in Hato Mayor, we attended a church called "Defender of the Faith," led by a Puerto Rican pastor, Domingo Uberia – the only pastor in the whole community able to speak English. The service had ended and I was getting onto the bus when Pastor Domingo called me back to the church. He told me that the next day all the pastors were going to meet in his home and he wondered if I could also come to the meeting.

I felt like I'd been hit with a ton of bricks. Yet I still resisted God, using the excuse that tomorrow I was going to visit the town prison. Pastor Domingo asked what time I was going and I told him I was going up in the morning and I would be back early afternoon. He said since they weren't meeting until four o'clock, I would have plenty of time. After that I had no excuse.

So when I got back from the prison I went to his house. All the pastors had gathered and were conversing in Spanish. There I sat, not understanding a word they were saying. I did, however, have my own conversation with God, assuring Him that this was not going to work.

They had been talking for perhaps ten minutes when suddenly everyone became quiet. Pastor Domingo looked at me and said, "The pastors want to know if you have anything you would like to tell us." I thought, *Oh boy, this is not going to be good.*

I hesitated for what seemed like minutes, although I'm sure it was only seconds. Finally I said, "You know, I have been praying for over a year about Hato Mayor and some thoughts keep coming to my mind. I didn't really want to share this with you but I think God is telling me to tell you something. I want you to remember I'm not a pastor like you but I'm just letting you know that I believe God is telling me to say something to you."

There was dead silence as I proceeded to explain that for over a year God had been urging me to come down and alert the pastors to get ready because there was going to be revival in their town. It took me a few minutes to get all this out because I was getting tears in my eyes. I thought maybe they would run me out of town, but instead they started jumping up and down, clapping and shouting and praising God. I was somewhat shocked by their enthusiasm. We stayed for perhaps two more hours and they formed a committee to organize and prepare for the revival God was going to send.

God was preparing for it, too. Later that week, about thirty minutes away in San Pedro, a very well-known Caribbean evangelist was holding a series of meetings in the parking lot of the country's largest baseball stadium. Attendance averaged close to twenty thousand a night. Some of the Hato Mayor pastors and I traveled to one of the services and arranged to meet with the evangelist afterward. As we talked together, he said God had been telling him that someone from another country would let him know where he was going to go preach in four months.

The evangelist agreed to come to Hato Mayor for a week, so we returned and began planning. I decided to buy five hundred index cards so pastors could get the names and addresses of people who were saved during the course of the week. When I returned to the States, I also bought one thousand "Steps to Peace with God" by Billy Graham in Spanish and took them back to the DR with me.

The pastors of Hato Mayor did all the planning. Churches organized big groups to pray 24-7 for this revival. At the local baseball stadium, a huge stage was built that stood approximately fifteen feet in the air, equipped with a sound system. The day before the revival began, the pastors organized a huge three-hour parade that involved perhaps 30,000 people in praying or watching or driving the huge dump trucks that played Christian music through special sound systems.

At noon on the first day, 150 people came to the stadium and prayed continually until 7:30 that night. One hundred ushers gathered to help out. People walked, they came on buses, they came in trucks, they came on motorcycles, mopeds, and bicycles, they came from towns that were twenty to thirty miles away. And by evening, the baseball stadium was packed - infield, outfield, and bleachers. I couldn't believe what I was seeing.

At the close of the first service, all the pastors came to the front and an altar call was given. That first night, the pastors gave out all five hundred cards we'd had for the week. In fact, they couldn't collect all the names of people who prayed to receive Christ; pastors were writing on pieces of paper. During that week, they collected over five thousand names of people who had prayed to receive Christ as their Savior. I sat and watched in utter amazement.

It was just a phenomenal experience. For me, it was a revelation of how big God is in this adventure we're on together. I'd had Him in a box, hoping and praying that we might get a few hundred cards filled out, and He exceeded my highest imagination by more than ten-fold.

Marcelino Cristian (Timan)
Another event happened that week. On the second day of the trip, Henry and I decided we needed to look for another place to stay because our mission groups were getting too large for the orphanage. So we went up to San Pedro, about thirty minutes away, to look at a facility there. Afterward, we boarded a bus that was going back to Hato Mayor. After we'd traveled about a mile, Henry realized that we had gotten on the wrong bus. This one stopped along the way; the one we wanted went straight through.

It was hot, over 100 degrees that day, and already mid-afternoon. I just wanted to go on to Hato Mayor, so I said, "Well, we'll just ride this bus."

What a mistake that was. For many miles, the bus stopped for everyone that was walking along the road. It was hot, and because we were sitting in the back of the bus, we got the fumes.

As we were riding, Henry tried to get me off the subject of the fumes and heat by telling me that down the road on the right was a Haitian village with a Christian and Missionary Alliance church in it. I tried to tell Henry there was no Christian and Missionary Alliance church there. I'd traveled that road dozens of times and there was no church.

He replied, "Oh yes, there is a church."

"No, there isn't," I insisted.

Finally (we were about half way to Hato Mayor) I said, "Henry, when we get to Hato Mayor, I am going to buy you an ice cream cone if there is a church in that village."

Within ten seconds, the bus stopped yet again and a short man boarded and walked back the aisle, passing empty seats to sit down beside me. After speaking to the man, Henry looked at me.

"You owe me an ice cream cone."

"What do you mean?" I asked.

"That's the pastor of the Christian and Missionary Alliance church that I was talking about," replied Henry.

"That can't be."

"Yes, that's the pastor".

So we struck up a conversation with the man. He was indeed the pastor and his name was Marcelino Cristian, later known to the Americans as Timan. Henry asked him where he was going. Timan said he was headed for a revival that was being held in the baseball stadium in Hato Mayor. He'd heard about an American who built churches, and he was going down to the revival hoping to find him because the roof had blown off his church and he needed help.

Henry informed Timan that I was the American he was hoping to find. The three of us had a nice conversation the rest of the way to Hato Mayor. I learned later that Timan, a Haitian, had walked to the DR from Haiti as a young witch doctor, had become a Christian, and had built a church to honor the God who saved him. He then went on to build eight more churches out in the surrounding sugar cane fields – the very churches we had rebuilt after the hurricane came through

On our next trip to the DR we did rebuild the roof on Timan's church. In fact, we changed our construction style at that point because one trip participant, Gary Renaud, owned a steel company. He showed us how we could tie the roof into the walls so that the trusses would not come up unless the whole structure was blown down. A hurricane went through the DR a year later and Timan's church had the only roof that lasted in that part of the country. That type of roof became very sought-after, and we've built numerous churches since then using the procedure we learned on Timan's church back in 1998.

Little did I know that Timan would eventually become the vice-president of the Christian and Missionary Alliance in the Dominican Republic and we would work together for the next fifteen years. Once again, God's planning was amazing.

*We were waiting a long time for the hand of God to move...
awaiting the tall, blue-eyed American that God had promised was going
to come. MGM has established the plan of God in Hato Mayor and,
especially for us, fulfilled His promise. MGM is for me the fulfillment of
God's promise.*

*The work that MGM does is extraordinary since it provides help
and support to the poorest, both Haitians and Dominicans, and anyone
who does not have access to the government resources. It helps soothe and
relieve peoples' lives. Not many are doing what MGM does – making lives
easier here on earth through simple things like giving a pair of glasses to
someone who can't afford them.*

*And because of MGM, Hato Mayor is seen as a more loving and
merciful community throughout the rest of the country.*

- Ada Barriola Lappot, Judge to the Dominican Republic

*Pastor Ondina died several years ago. I am her daughter and the
current pastor of the church she led. It was to her God promised a church
would be built across the Magua River on the edge of Hato Mayor.*

*At that time we were meeting in an open place and Jim came to
us and we recognized he was the one God had talked to my mother about
more than forty years ago. I've heard Jim testify that he had not intended
to come back, but he didn't have peace so he made another trip to build
Pastor Ondina a church.*

*I could see during the construction that Jim and his team did
everything with love and kindness. I watched closely and saw that they
were not just interested in building things and giving stuff to people, but
they really cared for those around us that had little.*

*As the pastor today, I want to let you know that we are fighting
to do the work of God. We want to remember and honor the effort of
all the people that have contributed to our church. We are expanding,
opening new churches and working with troubled youth – young people
into drugs and other problems. God has blessed us with a great group and
we already have great testimonies from them. And we owe all of that first
to God and then to MGM.*

- Damaris Barriola, Pastor of Sendas de Luz Church

*I remember the first time Jim McDonald came to our town,
about fifteen years ago. He came with the vision to make the kingdom
of God grow by supporting local churches. At the beginning it was only
the construction of churches. But now the work goes beyond lifting up
walls and roofs. I have seen a concern for the spiritual and theological*

preparation of those who have been called to the ministry and also those whose ministry is not so visible but is very important.

MGM has left an impact on the people in this town. The mission that God placed in Jim's hands through MGM has been executed. The main purpose of God is to save lives, and there are many people today serving the Lord in our churches because they have been touched by one of the missionaries who came with MGM. They have developed a very important work in Hato Mayor and in our country, and we expect God to continue to help our brother Jim and all those who have the responsibility of developing this work.

- Fernando Betancourt,
Pastor of The Second Church of God, M.I., Hato Mayor

I thank our Lord for calling me to the ministry of His Word. I remember being totally chained by the enemy. But on a Sunday in 1959 I visited a church and accepted Jesus Christ as my Savior. Then the Lord brought me to Experimental [Haitian village]. There I saw a great need and wanted to preach the gospel, but it wasn't until 1961, after I'd studied the Bible, been baptized, and gotten married, that I was given a church to pastor. I didn't think I had the capacity to do it, but I asked the Lord for wisdom and He has been helping me in a mighty way. That church has grown, as well as the other five or six churches I started for the glory of our Savior Jesus Christ. God has blessed me a lot, too. He gave me five children and now I have a family of fourteen grandchildren. I really don't know how to repay Him. May He continue to bless me and allow me to continue doing His work.

I remember a bus ride from San Pedro to Hato Mayor. On that ride, Henry introduced me to Jim and told him I was the pastor of Experimental, and Jim told Henry to ask me what the church needed. I replied that I was desperate because we had more rain falling inside the church than outside.

Jim made a commitment to visit me, and he did. The church roof was repaired and we are very grateful today for a job very well done. More than this, Jim's visit has been a great blessing to many other churches on the East Coast. Many churches were destroyed by Hurricane George, and with God and our brother Jim's help we were able to get many of them repaired. We are very thankful to the organization – brother Jim first, and all the workers coming with him, as well as our brother Arturo who keeps us informed and works lovingly with us in our region.

Jim is very interested in developing more leaders to help me in the work and he has just started a Bible Institute, with fourteen people in the first group. We believe this will be a great blessing for the church in this region. There are other towns needing more churches built that we haven't been able to reach yet, but we know that God will open more doors and windows, and with His help we'll be able to reach these places for the glory of God.

- Marcelino Cristians (Timan)

From Terry Young's journal on that first mission trip to rebuild churches that had been destroyed by Hurricane George (1998):

Saturday

Flew out of Erie at 2 am, left Pittsburgh at 6 am, arrived at Kennedy airport at 7:20. Left NY at 9 am and arrived at Santa Domingo at 1:45 pm. It was very crowded – took 2 hours to get our luggage.

We rode to Hato Mayor in the back of a truck – what a ride! We were stopped by police. The driver paid him 50 pesos and he let us go. That's how they earn enough money to support their families. Driving is crazy, four people on a little motorcycle.

We got to the orphanage where we will stay – very nice. We moved in, set up, and had our first DR meal. Later we walked up town for ice cream. Henry, who lives here and is our interpreter, knows where we can eat.

Went to bed after a cold shower. Slept good.

Sunday

Up with the roosters' crowing at 7 am. Had breakfast and walked to Nelson's dad's church. That was quite an experience. After lunch we met five Alliance missionaries. They gave us a cement mixer. Then we went to visit job sites – another incredible experience. The sugar cane fields measure 20 miles by 60 miles. It is impossible to describe the shacks people live in.

There are motorcycles everywhere – three or four people on one motorcycle, families with babies. I was elected to drive the truck this week. The people drive crazy – all over the road.

We went to Henry's church tonight. They really do worship the Lord here. An old lady in a wheelchair is the senior pastor. She had leprosy at age 22 and doctors sent her home to die; she is now 80-some. After church we went for ice cream. I drove the truck with everyone in back. It's a real trip driving in town. No lights.

Came back to orphanage and got supplies ready for tomorrow. 11:30 – good night.

Monday

We had to pick up mortar, and I watched how they make block. We started laying blocks about 10:30 and worked till 5:30. The kids hung around us all day. They watch us eat lunch, which gives us a funny feeling. We laid about 600 blocks. The church we're working on is 20 ft. by 40 ft., 7 courses with 3 doors.

Came home and ate supper. We were very tired, but went to Rev. Reveres' church. That was like a camp meeting, Church of God style. Wasn't over till 10:00 pm.

Tuesday

Partly cloudy, nice breeze, in the 80's. We got a good start at 9 am and finished our work at 3 pm. We had fun with the Haitian kids. Henry, Adam and I went to get lumber – 15) 16' x 1" and 2) 12'6" boards. Henry bartered - $246 American dollars..

We went to a Haitian church tonight. They really sing. Dad had a little Haitian girl sitting beside him. After church we went for ice cream. To bed at 11:00.

Wednesday

Up early and off to the bush. We laid 8 courses on a church where the preacher is 73 years old and cuts sugar cane all day. We finished work at 5:30 and played with the kids a couple hours, then the truck came to pick us up. We had a late supper and didn't go to church.

Dad is having a great time. Adam is laying block and having a great time, too. I'm glad I brought him. He's a nice boy. Right now he's playing with a frog and everyone is laughing. It's 11:00 and we're trying to go to sleep.

Thursday

The temperature hasn't been too bad, some clouds and a nice breeze. Has rained every day. My truck has no horn and no wipers – it's very hard to see the DR people at night in the rain. We worked very hard on the second church, then went back to the first church to finish it. Adam is working like a trooper; I am very proud of him. We have one church ready for a roof.

The Haitian people are very nice and some like to help. The kids are very cute and you never hear them crying. The hardest part is eating lunch while they watch. We feed the men that help, but we can't feed them all.

Our group is working together really well and God is really blessing everyone.

Friday
>   Up early – the roosters wake me up. We worked on Henry's house. It was nice to be outside of town on a hill by ourselves – no people around and a clean site. We got the little house ready for scaffolding and went back to the orphanage for lunch, then took a little nap because it was raining.
>   In the evening we went to a small church outside of town. Jim preached and Henry interpreted, and two fellows accepted Jesus into their hearts. We got ice cream after church. Dad didn't go – he's resting up for the long trip home. I talked to Patti. I miss her very much – can't wait to see her.

Saturday
>   We finished the block work on the second church – that was our goal. The 73-year old preacher really got to our hearts. Dad took him a new T-shirt and a bag of candy. I gave him my work boots. Dad gave all the kids candy. They were laughing and happy – it was very hard to leave. Adam gave his work boots to Magill, the Dominican master builder that helped us. I would like to bring him to the States and teach him our way of masonry.
>   About 1 pm we left for the ocean to swim and relax. The water was very nice and warm.

Sunday
>   It's about 5:30 am and the roosters are crowing. We'll leave for the airport in a few hours. It's been a real experience for the three of us. Can't wait to see Patti and take a hot shower!

4

A PLACE TO CALL HOME

New Ministries

More and more people were joining us on mission trips. This was partly because my son, Dr. Michael McDonald, a general practitioner from Slippery Rock, had become interested in what we were doing. In 1998 he purchased a bit of medicine and, joined by a couple of nurses, headed up our first medical team in the Dominican Republic. After he saw the situation, he returned the following year with several other doctors and a larger supply of medicine.

Today the medical team has grown from a handful of people to closer eighty to ninety participants and includes nurses, pharmacists, doctors and nurse practitioners from across the United States. We now run

Jim and a Friend

multiple mission trips each year and bring physicians on nearly every trip, along with hundreds of thousands of dollars worth of medicine annually. God has truly blessed our medical team and made it a blessing to literally thousands of Haitians and Dominicans, and we are grateful.

As we searched in 1998 for a place to house our growing ministry, we visited a compound owned by Tony Fernandez, a professional baseball player who had played for the Cleveland Indians and was a Christian. He held summer programs at his Dominican facility. We talked to him about housing arrangements, and the following year we left the orphanage in Hato Mayor and moved to his compound where there was plenty of room for us.

Also, after I came back from the 1998 trips I went to visit my brother, Russ, in California. His two sons, Rusty and Jeff, had been professional baseball players; Rusty had pitched for the Dodgers and Jeff had pitched for the Seattle Mariners. My nephews listened to me sharing about mission trips, and before I returned to Pennsylvania they mentioned they would like to come along on one just to see what it was like in the DR.

So in 1999 Rusty and Jeff came on their first trip and stayed at Tony Fernandez' place. They worked a little bit of construction, but one day they got a group of Dominican boys together and started giving them some baseball pointers. The next thing they knew, they had two hundred kids around them. As a result, they decided to come back the next year and, instead of doing construction, travel to various places and talk about baseball. Before they returned the following year, Henry had found four or five different locations for them to visit.

From that time on, God has really honored the baseball ministry. Forty to fifty people now serve on our "baseball team." On a typical day they travel to a village or town and hold morning and afternoon sessions focused on baseball. Each session averages 250-400 kids. One member of the team shares the gospel after each session, and they hand out Bibles and Bible tracts to anyone who wants to receive Christ. They have distributed several thousand Bibles. Baseball is an incredible draw in the DR and to have American professional baseball players come down and share the gospel with them is almost unbelievable to them.

The team has since brought with them several other men who have played professional baseball. They've also brought coaches from colleges and high schools in California, Pennsylvania, and Ohio. Both American and Dominican coaches have received a great blessing from these trips, as have the many young people who attended and responded to the gospel.

This ministry continues to evolve. In 2006 they held their first Coaches Conference. Coaches from California went to the DR and held a three-day conference, teaching 45 Dominican coaches how to be a Christian coach in the Dominican Republic. It, too, proved to be a major blessing, so another conference was held the next year with 95 coaches in attendance. They're now considering plans to hold two back-to-back, three-day conferences, anticipating one hundred coaches at each conference.

A Place of Our Own

In 1998, after prayerfully considering our options, we finally determined that we were going to build our own facility. Tony Fernandez' compound was a good temporary solution, but we were thinking toward the future. So we started looking around for a good location.

Meanwhile, Henry Mercedes (who was now working for us full time) and his wife, Rhodie, were living in one room above his father's restaurant in Hato Mayor. Henry's wife wanted to move out of town, but I tried to discourage this, urging them to locate in town where they could walk to everything. Rhodie, however, was unswayed. Furthermore, she had already picked out the lot!

So we started to build a house for them on the lot she had purchased about a mile out of town. I visited the work site one day and walked behind the construction and up to the top of a little hill. When I turned around, I could see the whole valley and the entire town of Hato Mayor. It was a gorgeous view, with scarcely anyone around except the house we were building.

It came to me, then, that this was exactly where God wanted us to build the center for our organization. I could envision it as plain as day. So I went down and brought all the workers up and had them look at it too, and they all admired the view. Not only was the site beautiful, it also provided a rock foundation so that our mission center would stand firm in the fierce Dominican hurricanes. And it was elevated, so we wouldn't have standing water that would attract mosquitoes and other insects. Clearly, God had put this location in Henry's wife's heart, and through her led us to the site for our MGM center.

I went home and started making some drawings and thinking and praying and planning and talking to construction people as well as to many others. By early 1999, we started sending groups to begin the two-year construction of the new facility.

On one of those trips, we'd brought mostly block layers and construction workers, along with a children's ministry team and some wives to help with cooking. We stayed at Tony Fernandez' compound and commuted over to the worksite on the other side of Hato Mayor.

We had planned a one-floor facility, but as the workers were sitting in the dirt eating lunch one day, one of the men said,

"You know, why don't you put a second floor on this?"

I replied, "I'm not sure whether we are going to have enough money to put the roof on the first floor let alone add a second floor."

Someone suggested, "Why don't you put some rooms up there where people could come and stay?"

I said, "That might be a nice idea too, but, again, it's a problem of money".

"What do you think one of these rooms would cost?" I was asked. "I have no idea."

As we ate our lunch, the block layers started figuring, and came up with a cost of approximately $4,500 to 5,000 per room. To my amazement, a number of people who were sitting around us said they would donate that amount of money if they could have a place up on the second floor. Sitting together in the dirt that day, we raised all the money for materials to build nine apartments on the second floor.

We came back the following year and added the second floor, with the understanding that contributors could use it as a tax deduction and anytime they came on a mission trip, they could stay in their room (when they weren't there, the room was available for others to use). In this way, we were able to fund the second floor and roof at no cost to our organization.

On that second floor we now have nine apartments including two with private bathrooms, general bathrooms, and a chapel or "Upper Room" that seats 150-175 people and offers a gorgeous view of the valley. That is where we come to see the sunrise every morning. Downstairs we have 104 beds, a large dining area, a kitchen, a storage room, a pharmacy, and a veranda. It is a beautiful facility that has been given to us by God, who had His hand in it all. He had the right people there at the right time and gave a worker an idea, and as a result we doubled the capacity of the facility that we were building for Him.

MGM Center Mural in the Upper Room

A Mountaintop Experience

In 2000, while we were still based at Tony Fernandez' compound and ours was being built, a unique event occurred. Close to one hundred people had come along on this particular trip, including baseball players from California and people from Ohio and various other states. We'd had a great week and had come down to the last night, which has always, since the beginning of this operation, had a special significance. On that last night, everyone gathers together to share what God has shown them during the course of the week.

This time, Tim Feathers, a pastor from Fairlawn Alliance Church, suggested we hold a communion service. A lady who had been to India brought a candle that had been on seven different continents, and we added other candles, enough so each person would have one to light and later take back to their respective churches and homes.

We started our sharing time at 7:30 p.m., and what happened was one of the most unusual experiences I have seen on a mission trip. First we had the communion service. When it ended, we lit a single candle and then went around and lit everyone else's candle. Several people prayed, and this led into a time of singing and praying that lasted for a couple of hours.

Then we blew out the candles and started sharing. As we did, phenomenal things began to happen. One fellow stepped forward and prophesied over us, telling us what he thought God had told him was going to happen in the future. Many there remembered what he said, and saw it come true a few years later.

Normally, our sharing time would last an hour or two. But this night, we'd started at 7:30 p.m., and were still going at 4:00 a.m. Nobody went to bed; in fact, people ran to the bathroom and back because they were afraid they were going to miss something. God worked in a phenomenal way among us. The reason the meeting finally ended at 4:00 a.m. was because the bus arrived to take the California contingent to the airport. Of course they hadn't even packed yet, so they had to hurry to get ready to leave and the sharing time came to an end.

Years later, we still talk about that night. Many people remember the awesome things that happened the night sharing started at 7:30 in the evening and concluded at 4:00 the next morning.

The Finishing Touch

Our retreat center was completed in 2001 and we based our first mission trip there that year. We began to grow in size again through the blessings of God – but we still lacked something. We didn't have a name.

Chris Palmer, a young man from Zelienople, Pa., accompanied us in 2001. He'd been on other trips with us and now heard we were trying to come up with a name for our organization. After he went back home, he sent me a drawing of an MGM logo, with "Meeting God in Missions" printed below. He thought this would be a good name for the organization because he himself had met God in a life-changing way on one of our trips. He'd heard of many others, who had come down to help the Dominicans and Haitians and instead were helped themselves as God met them there and transformed them.

So through a young man from Zelienople, Pennsylvania, God gave our organization a name: Meeting God in Missions.

MGM Center

This is the centerpiece of the MGM Center

In November of 1999, Jim McDonald visited his brother Russell and nephew Jeff McDonald in California. Jim shared about the mission trips he'd been leading to the Dominican Republic and invited Jeff (a friend of mine) to join him on one.

Jeff was excited, and called me the next day to tell me we were going to the DR to build some churches. Jeff didn't give me any choice, so I agreed!

Jeff has a passion for baseball. He, his brother, and his dad had all played Major League ball. He'd also been involved with Baseball Chapel at that level and loved serving God through the sport whenever he could. Jeff and I had been coaching baseball together for ten years, using it as an outreach ministry.

Jeff had experienced first-hand the Dominican passion for baseball when he played in the Minor Leagues in Latin America, and he decided we should do a Baseball Clinic during our week in the DR, after the construction work was completed. In preparation, we gathered as much baseball equipment as possible to take with us to give out to the players and coaches.

That first trip took place in January of 2000. We worked construction all week, and on our last day we held one Baseball Clinic. Afterward, we shared the Bible message with all the players and coaches. It was such a success that in 2001 we traveled around the island and held clinics all week. The Baseball Ministry was now officially started.

This past January, 2010, marked our eleventh annual January trip. We've conducted over seventy clinics, involved over 10,000 players, and have given out hundreds of duffle bags containing new and used baseball equipment. We have shared the message of salvation with these players and coaches, and have given out thousands of tracts and Bibles. And we have prayed with thousands of them to receive Jesus Christ as their Savior and Lord.

After the first few years, Jeff and I realized we needed a Dominican man, strong in character and knowledgeable about baseball, to be our point man throughout the year – someone who would set up clinics and handle the equipment in an honest way. We asked for God's guidance and provision.

In 2000, during our very first baseball clinic, we had met a fourteen-year-old boy named Ramon Castro. After the message, Ramon came up to me and told me was already a Christian. The spirit of God was shining through his face. He left an incredible impression on me, and I wrote his name down in my journal as a reminder to pray for him. Actually, God had me write his name down so I would know, when our paths crossed again five years later, that His plan was coming together.

Sometime after that first clinic, Ramon had gone to New York to live with his aunt and attend high school there. He was drafted by the Chicago White Sox but turned down the offer in order to attend college, something he'd promised his mother he would do. During his first freshman semester in college he did well in school and in baseball. But in December of 2004 he was deported back to the Dominican on a technicality for not making a visit back home.

One month later, at our first clinic of the 2005 trip, we found ourselves short on translators. Jeff yelled into the crowd, asking if there was anyone who could speak English. One young man raised his hand and Jeff called him forward. Guess who... Ramon Castro! We didn't put it all together until the next evening when we were talking with him at the camp (he'd changed a lot in five years). As we talked, I opened my journal to 2000, and there was his name: "Ramon Castro."

Ramon had a Christian friend named Luis Silvestre who was also a very good baseball player. These two young men became God's answer to our prayer – His point men for the baseball ministry in the Dominican. Jeff and I hadn't envisioned men quite this young, but it was obviously God's intention. Ramon and Luis have done a great job and the work has gone very well. They have proven to be trustworthy and God has blessed them with His strength and wisdom. It has been an inspiration to Jeff and I to work with them. This experience has also increased my confidence that God is always at work, even when we aren't seeing results with our own eyes.

While we were in the DR for the annual player clinics in January of 2007, we met a Dominican named Pedro. Pedro had been in the United States for 24 years and played Major League baseball there. He'd made the forty man roster a few times but never made it permanently. When we met Pedro he had only been back in the Dominican for one week. He'd returned to follow a call from God to minister to the Dominicans through baseball. As it turned out he was good friends with Ramon's family and had played baseball with Ramon's uncle in the United States. Ramon remembered him from childhood and said he was a good man. When I shared the vision God had given us for the baseball ministry, Pedro began to cry tears of joy and said, "Thank you Lord." Then he told us, "God gave me that same vision and told me He would send a man to help me with this work."

While Pedro was in the States, we learned, he had started working with the drug cartel from Latin America and was making so much money that he gave up baseball. He was caught and sentenced to a 120-year prison term. While he was in prison, God got a hold of his heart and transformed him. God used Pedro in a mighty way, through him transforming not only many individual lives for eternity, but also the culture of the whole prison. His worked was recognized by the Warden and Pedro was asked to serve on several statewide and national committees for prison reform while serving his time. As a result, the Governor eventually commuted his sentence. Pedro is currently the Leader of the Meeting God in Baseball Ministry in the Dominican and works with Ramon and Luis in carrying out the work of the vision throughout the year.

In 2001 we began to realize that we needed a way to disciple each coach and player who prayed to receive Christ at the clinics. For several years we tried connecting with local churches and pastors for follow-up, but that just didn't work out. Then God laid it on our hearts to start discipling the baseball coaches so they in turn could disciple the players. Our goal was to train coaches in both baseball and discipleship skills.

So in May of 2007 my wife Phyllis and I went to the Dominican and traveled around the island with Ramon, Luis and Pedro. We visited six different cities and talked with fifty baseball coaches about doing Coaches Clinics for the purposes mentioned above. Enthusiasm was high; it was clearly time to launch this new phase of our ministry.

Headed home on the airplane, I prayed about what U.S. coaches we should invite to teach at the first Coaches Clinic. God gave me the name of a very successful baseball coach, John Diatte, from Valley Christian High School. John is a man of God and his teams are usually top-ranked in California and nationally.

We arrived home, and the next morning I went to church. I hadn't seen John in a number of years, but as the service concluded and I turned to leave, John was right behind me, looking right at me. I immediately asked him if he would like to go on a missions trip to the Dominican to hold a baseball clinic with a spiritual emphasis. He looked at me, puzzled, and immediately said yes. He then shared that God had been working on him pretty hard to get involved in some short term missions trip, but he'd had no idea how to do that. We talked things over and John agreed to take on the task of assembling our "team" of American Coaches. Because of his involvement in local, state and national coaches' associations, the job was a great fit for him.

In October, 2007, we conducted our first annual Coaches Baseball and Discipleship Clinic. By our third clinic in 2009, we had 120 Dominican coaches in attendance. These are generally three-day clinics, during which Dominican coaches are brought to the MGM facility and fed, housed, and loved on while receiving a balance of baseball training and spiritual instruction.

I will never forget how the Dominican coaches starting celebrating that first year when we announced one night we were going to show them a movie on the big screen, using the PC projector from their training classes. And when they heard we were going to serve them popcorn during the movie - they actually started jumping up and down and dogpiling on top of *each other! To see these grown men celebrating over movie and popcorn like they just won the World Series is a memory that I will cherish forever.*

In January of 2010 we held our first discipleship-only clinic. It was attended by thirty-five of the most committed Dominican coaches, men who have been diligently carrying out the Meeting God in Baseball vision throughout the year with their players. With God's help we plan to do more of these, and to begin discipleship retreats for the players also. In addition, Pedro, Ramon and Luis travel to various cities throughout the year, providing ongoing discipleship for the coaches.

On a more personal level...

During that first trip in January, 2000, I experienced an incredible peace in my heart. I didn't realize that it was, as Jim says, the beginning of discovering and getting into God's "movie" for my life. The trips since then haven't always been easy, but I always experience that same peace in my heart while I am there, and I always experience a special communion with the Lord through the power of the Holy Spirit.

In my early years as a Christian, God had allowed me to experience some incredible blessings as I served Him for His purposes. After three years, however, that ministry work abruptly ended and I spent the next fifteen years walking in the desert, searching my soul and crying out to God, asking Him to show me how to get peace and blessing back in my life. I experienced some tough personal challenges, and at the end of this fifteen-year period I had lost most of my hope. My heart was full of despair. I couldn't even pray anymore; all I could get out was, "Help me, Jesus, help me." Little did I know that was all I really needed to pray. Little did I know that He'd always been with me, always loving me, and continually blessing me even through the hard times and personal challenges.

Looking back, I am convinced that God allowed me to experience those incredible blessings in my early years so I would remember them while going through the tough experiences that would prepare me for this work in the Dominican Republic. I praise God now for that fifteen-year walk in the desert, and I wouldn't trade that experience for anything.

On my very first missions trip, I knew that God had something for me in the Dominican and I knew I had to continue coming back each year - if only to experience that incredible peace in my heart and those special times with Him. In those early years I was still healing, but ultimately, by spending more of my time focusing on this ministry each year, my peace of heart has become continuous and steady.

- Don Schulz, San Jose, CA

FOLLOWING GOD INTO HAITI

In 1999 I received another call from the Christian and Missionary Alliance headquarters in Colorado Springs. Fred Smith, who was in charge of worldwide missions for the C&MA, had heard of the work we'd done rebuilding the churches in the sugar cane fields a few years earlier.

Fred explained that the C&MA was interested in planting churches in the country of Haiti. They needed someone to go down and begin building the churches in preparation for their evangelization effort there. He wanted to know if I would be interested in flying to Haiti to meet him and Brav Lavador, a Haitian who currently lived in Atlanta, Georgia. The three of us would look at locations that were potentially suitable for the construction of the first Christian and Missionary Alliance church in Haiti. I prayed about this opportunity, and later called Fred back and agreed to meet him in Haiti and spend a week scouting out sites for churches.

So in the spring of 1999, the three of us met and visited possible sites in and around Port-au-Prince, Haiti's capital city. Then Brav rented a vehicle and he and I spent a day traveling over three mountain ranges to reach Cap Haitien, a city located on Haiti's northern coast, where Brav had grown up.

By the end of the week, it became apparent to me that it would be difficult to build a church in Port-au-Prince. Each day our large construction crew would have to spend nearly four hours in travel just to get from our lodging to the work site and back. Not only would we be losing valuable construction time, but we'd also be traveling under very dangerous conditions.

Cap Haitien, however, was more rural and much less congested. We looked at several sites there over a two- or three-day period, and came to an agreement. We would build a facility for the C&MA outside of Cap Haitien on a peninsula that jutted out into the Atlantic Ocean.

Brav and I returned and met with Fred Smith. It was agreed that I would gather a mission team, do some fundraising, and take the workers to the Cap Haitien area to build this facility.

I came back home and, six months later, assembled a construction team of approximately twenty-five people. Three days before we were scheduled to leave, I hadn't heard anything from the Christian and Missionary Alliance. So I called the headquarters and contacted Fred Smith to tell him we were leaving to build this church. That's when I learned that someone was supposed to have contacted me several months earlier. The C&MA had determined that they were not going to go into Haiti. Through some mix-up, I hadn't received that message, and we now had a group of people with airplane tickets to Haiti, ready to build a church.

Cebien Alexis

We decided to go anyway, and a few days later we boarded the airplane for Haiti. Arrangements had been made for us to stay with the Davis family, missionaries who lived outside of Cap Haitien.

Once we were situated, we went out to the work site where we were to build the church. In talking with the local pastor, however, we found that he would rather have a school than a church. Since we were no longer connected with the Alliance on this project, we decided to go ahead and honor his wishes and start a school. But I struggled to understand why God had seemed to call us to go to Haiti in the first place, yet when we went things appeared to fall apart. Through it all, I kept praying and trying to understand what God wanted us to do.

The first evening we were there, the workers wanted to go out and attend church somewhere, just as we did in the Dominican. The missionaries didn't want us to go because they didn't think it was safe. Most of my crew, however, were construction workers who felt they were capable of taking care of themselves, and they still wanted to go.

The first night, we stayed in and fellowshipped together. On the second night, as we were finishing up supper, the guys were razzing me a little bit about why we weren't going to church. So I went into the bedroom, alone, and started praying and again asking God what was going on. I felt he had called us here, yet we were struggling. The guys wanted to go to church, our hosts didn't want to go to church, and I wanted to go but felt I had to honor the wishes of the people with whom we were staying. So I was trying to understand what God was telling me.

During my prayer time, one of the men came to my room and said there was somebody outside who wanted to see me. I had no idea who it could be - I knew no one there. I walked out into the dining area where everyone was still talking together, and over by the door stood a tall, dark Haitian. I went over and introduced myself to him. Amazingly, he spoke English. He introduced himself as Cebien Alexis. He was a pastor and a physician, and he'd come just to say hello, find out if everything was going alright, and see if there was anything he could do or get for us.

We chatted together and I invited him to stay awhile, but he said he had other engagements. After perhaps half an hour, he got ready to leave, saying, "If there is nothing I can do for you, then I am going to go."

As he turned around to walk out the door, I believe the Holy Spirit reminded me that I had been asking Him to provide a place for us to go to church. So I stopped Cebien as he opened the door, and I said,

"You know, there is something you can do for us. All these people are used to going to church at night, and the missionaries don't feel it's safe. You wouldn't happen to know any church around here that would be safe for us to attend?"

He looked at me and said, "Would you like to go to one of mine?"

I thought his wording was strange, so I asked him, "How many do you have?"

He replied, "Well, I have over one hundred."

I thought, *Man, you have over one hundred churches.*

He said, "I have been building churches and training pastors. As a matter of fact, I am going tonight to the church where I pastor. We are having a service."

"Is there any chance we could go with you?"

He said there was, and he could rent us a truck and take the rest of us in his vehicle. So we determined that we would eat early and just as soon as we got through eating he would come by and take us down to his church.

After supper Cebien arrived. We jumped in the truck and his car and away we went to Cap Haitien, probably five or six miles away.

That short trip was an eye-opener for all of us. We saw unbelievable sights - dead animals along the road, funeral processions, filth, garbage, and staggering poverty. Every human being you saw was in need. They were starving to death, they were congregated along the sides of the road because there was no work and nothing to do. Many tin huts had been built on the bare mountainsides surrounding Cap Haitien, and heavy rains regularly washed the sewage from these huts down into troughs that ran along the road. It was a deplorable situation.

We arrived at the church and had an interesting service. We found that Haitian believers worship God with a lot of passion and they love to sing. When the meeting was over, we started back to the missionaries' home. As I rode with Cebien, he began telling me a little bit about his life.

Cebien's mom, a Haitian living in England, had brought his brother and him to Haiti when he was two years old. Cebien became a Christian and had been serving God for many years. He was now a physician, and had also started purchasing land throughout the country (a section of land could be bought for one American dollar). He would build a church on the land he'd purchased, and then give the property back to the community. He'd built over one hundred churches, but right now, on his blackboard at home, he had a list of thirty-nine additional locations where people were requesting a church to be built.

"Would you like to see some of them?" he asked. So the next day five of us got in his vehicle and went around the countryside looking at places that needed churches built or completed, or needed a tree limb school built.

Cebien operated dozens of tree limb schools. He educated and paid the salaries of one teacher per school, and these teachers taught a combined total of 6,600 students. The schools were built by cutting tree limbs and using them as a framework, then cutting more limbs to make trusses for a roof which was then covered with palm leaves. The floor was dirt and there were no walls. Students sat on makeshift benches. Most of the schools didn't have a blackboard.

That was their version of school. We stopped and saw one and, needless to say, our hearts were touched.

Cebien's Dream

As we toured the sites with Cebien, I began to think, *Maybe this is why God brought us here. Not for the Christian Missionary and Alliance after all, but to join up with this fellow and help in building churches or whatever God calls us to do.*

As we were concluding the day, while I rode along trying to pray and process it all, Cebien said he wanted to show us something that wasn't even listed on his board, something that had been his dream for years, although it seemed to be impossible. "It" was located near his home.

Cebien lived at an orphanage that he'd had built about twenty-five years ago. At this orphanage also lived two Christian ladies who had been there with him all that time, teaching kindergarten through possibly sixth grade.

Just before we reached the orphanage we turned onto a dirt road, traveled about a mile and a half along the ocean, and pulled onto a path that went out into a field of perhaps twenty-some acres. Huge trees grew on it, which was unusual in that part of the country. One side was bordered by large and beautiful mansions enclosed by walls with wrought iron gates. These, we were informed, were the homes of drug dealers.

"Well, what is this?" I asked as we looked around the property. Cebien replied, "This is the dream I have - to build a university." His dream, he explained, came out of his conviction that the only way the Haitian people can be rescued from the plight they are in is through education.

Cebien gave us some background on Haiti's situation. He told us that on January 1, 1800, the Haitian government had signed a one-hundred-year pact to worship the devil and make voodoo their national religion. In 1900, they renewed the pact for the next one hundred years. The population throughout that period of time was comprised mostly of devil worshippers who had come from Africa through the slave trade.

In the 1900s, missionaries started coming to Haiti and many people in the country became Christian. Now there were many evangelical denominations in the country of Haiti, with a lot of missionaries trying to bring about change. Still, the people struggled to get away from their past.

We listened, trying to grasp the scenario, as Cebien shared his vision for this university. Then we got back in the car, returned to our living quarters, and started discussing the possibility of coming back the following year to help Cebien. As the construction crew joined us and learned of the situation, they unanimously thought it was a good idea. So we all committed to pray about it and see if God would affirm our coming back.

Every night Cebien came to take us to a church for evening

worship, and we really had some adventures. It was much different than the Dominican Republic. Sometimes church was held in the middle of fields, sometimes in roads - sometimes it was held in intersections! At the conclusion of each service there was an altar call, and I think every night there were people saved.

The people themselves were much different than those in the Dominican Republic because although both were needy, the Haitians' poverty was more severe and they were desperate and without hope. They were reduced to one meal every two days and their children were starving to death right in front of them. They were searching and trying to find comfort and a way to get out of these conditions, and when offered hope and a future, they were very receptive. I could see why the gospel was spreading in Haiti.

A couple of months after our trip, I contacted everybody that had gone with us and told them I believed God wanted us to go back. We were going to, of all things, start building a university in Haiti.

Faith Christian University

The following year, 2000, we traveled to Haiti to begin work on the university.

It was a six-year project. The first two years, we scheduled the trips in November because that suited our schedules – not realizing that was monsoon rain time! The rains came off the ocean and beat on the tin roof at night. It might rain five or six inches during the night, leaving us to work in six to eight inches of mud during the day. In fact, one week they calculated forty-two inches of rainfall. We would try to bring in cement block only to have the trucks get buried in the mud. Then we would have to unload the blocks from the trucks, push the trucks out of the mud, and load the blocks back in. It was a nightmare. After those first two years, the trips were moved to February and April. We were delighted to find that it hardly rained during those months and we could even walk on the ground without sinking – a real blessing!

Construction in Haiti presented challenges, not only in the area of weather but also in methods and available material. For instance, to obtain sand for mortar, one Haitian would dig the sand out of a river bed, another would throw it halfway up the hill, a third would shovel it to the top, and a fourth man would load it into a truck. So the sand we used to mix the concrete had already been shoveled four times by Haitians. They were eager, though, to work for five or six dollars a day because normally they would be paid two dollars.

Also, once we'd committed to the project, Cebien bought a little block form and hired a young man to make blocks, one at a time, ten hours a day, six days a week. Then, despite the monsoon rains, we had to haul them to the construction site. It was hard work for everybody.

We had decided to build an American-style university. There was nothing like this in the country of Haiti. Usually an entire university - classrooms, offices, everything – was housed under one roof. Ours would have separate facilities.

Our first project was a twelve-classroom building that looked somewhat like a two-story hotel. It took us two years to complete this large building. I vividly remember how difficult it was getting the blocks to the second level, mixing mortar up there, and meeting many other challenges in the course of the project.

At the end of two years, the facility, with six classrooms on each floor, was ready. Cebien had it finished off, with a beautiful veranda and steps up to the second floor. He had a smooth finish put on the outside walls, and added the final touches. When we came back, it was absolutely gorgeous, with hallways ten feet wide and steps twelve feet wide, complete with pillars and rails. Cebien did a marvelous job of making the building look special.

The following year we started construction on a dormitory that would house about one hundred students. We made the beds in the United States and shipped them over in containers, along with computers and other things the university needed.

At the conclusion of six years, we had built the twelve-classroom building, the dormitory, and a library fully furnished with books in Spanish and Creole. Over the library was a computer center with fifty computers and a server. We'd built a cafeteria and a kitchen with a large walk-in refrigerator, and constructed an eight-apartment complex for teachers, furnished with beds, dressers, fans and lights (this facility also included a large conference room). And Cebien had another structure built that would house three families, for those teachers who brought spouses and children with them.

The university began to operate while we were finishing up some of the buildings. There were startup problems of various kinds, and in the midst of all of this, security in Haiti became very tenuous. People were being kidnapped, travel was becoming treacherous, and our State Department frequently put out warnings to Americans. In time we grew concerned about the safety issue and about the university's difficulty in gaining accreditation.

So in 2006, we determined we would wait until conditions improved before returning to continue our work in Haiti. Currently we await God's leading. Many Americans who went on those trips want to go back and work in Haiti again. I hope that at some point, in God's time, He will open the doors for us to return, and that when he does the university will have gained its accreditation and be moving ahead. Our experience there certainly was a blessing, and God's hand was in it all.

Haiti Highlights

During our six years there, we had some of the greatest encounters with God that most of us have ever experienced in our lifetime. Two of these experiences happened as we went out to visit churches in Haiti.

The first happened the second year we were there. We were getting a little more confident and we told Cebien we would like to go to a worship service in a remote area, just to see what was happening out there. So one night we all packed into one truck, bound for such a place.

Don, the missionary, drove, while Cebien sat in the middle and I sat by the passenger door. All of the construction workers rode standing in the back of the truck. We traveled several dirt roads for perhaps ten to fifteen miles, then turned off into a grass field and continued probably ten miles or more. It was dark by the time we came to a dried-up riverbed perhaps one hundred yards wide. In the rainy season this area is flooded by rainwater which runs off the high mountains around Cap Haitien. It had eroded the sides of the riverbed until the bank was about a four-foot drop-off. Cebien knew we needed to cross it to get to the church (still about five miles from that point), but he wasn't sure where the crossing was located

As we drove along the riverbed, anxiety building, Don considered trying to take the truck over the four-foot embankment. From my vantage point, I could see that if we tried to do that, it would total the truck and endanger us all. I urged, "Don, you need to stop and look over here, because there is a large drop-off, straight down into the riverbed, and there is no way your truck is going to survive this."

We drove a bit further, and Don again stopped and considered trying to cross. As we talked, my truck window open because of the heat, I heard a voice outside, and looked out.

Standing beside the riverbed were two Haitians. One asked, "Are you having trouble, do you need help?" I couldn't believe that we had traveled along the riverbed for miles, and when we finally stopped, two Haitians stood nearby – one of them English-speaking. The people in the back of the truck listened as I replied,

"Yes, we are trying to get to a church but we don't know how to get across the riverbed."

"Would you like me to help you?" he asked.

"That would really be appreciated."

"Okay, just follow me." He and his companion started walking along the riverbed. As we drove alongside the men, Don pulled ahead until they were slightly behind my door.

We hadn't gone more than fifty yards when our guide said, "Right here is where you cross." We had been looking for that spot for thirty minutes! I looked over to Don, "Don, right up here is where we are going to cross the riverbed." Then I turned back to thank the two men, and there was no one there. I couldn't believe it.

I told Don and Cebien, "You know what, there is nobody out there." Yet we had heard the voices; we had seen the guys standing there; we had been led to the crossing.

We crossed the riverbed and went to the church. It was a small church with about three hundred people in attendance. By the light of an old lantern, Cebien played "Amazing Grace" on his accordion, and we all sang and praised the Lord together. Then we came home and talked about our travel experience. And I think to a man, everyone believed that God sent those Haitians to help us get across the riverbed that night. Today, I am sure all of us remember that situation like it happened yesterday.

The second experience took place the fifth year we were in Haiti. Cebien told us he wanted to take us to another remote church, a trip of forty-five to fifty minutes. It was a Sunday and we left right after lunch, planning to attend the service and be back for a late dinner around seven o'clock.

After traveling awhile, we passed through a good-sized village. On the far side of it we entered a barrio with literally thousands of huts strung out along both sides of a wide riverbed which we needed to cross. These huts were constructed of cardboard, tin, tree limbs, baked mud, or whatever else they could find.

Vacation Bible School

We drove down into the riverbed and had nearly made it to the other side when we hit a wet area and the truck got stuck. We all got out of the truck to push. That's when we noticed that the large crowd of Haitians who had followed our progress through town, and congregated perhaps half a mile away to watch us, were now running toward us.

I thought they were running to help us, but all those in the back of the truck thought they were running to harm us. Needless to say, our people hollered to the driver to push on the gas. Mud and rocks and water flew and the Americans were getting covered with dirt, but no one complained because they were anxious to get the truck moving.

With the Haitians coming closer all the time, the truck slowly began to move and our people hurried to jump back on it. After we got the truck going, the Haitians stopped and walked back towards the village.

It was pitch-dark when, an hour and a quarter later, we arrived at the field where the service was being held. The people were all waiting for us. Their church was about six- by eight-feet, with a roof of tree limbs covered with palm leaves. There was one bench. The place was so small that most of the Haitians had to stand outside.

As the meeting began, Cebien asked me to say a few words. The pulpit area was furnished with a little nightstand and on it stood an old oil lantern which the leader stands beside to read the Bible. So Cebien and I stood together, and I read in English while he translated in Creole. At the conclusion, we had twenty to twenty-five adults and children who accepted Christ.

Then we all said good bye, concerned because we were supposed to have been back for dinner by seven o'clock. It was half past seven and we were just now starting home, so we knew the cooks would be worrying.

We finally sat down to dinner at ten o'clock that night, laughing and joking about "Were they coming after us to harm us when we got stuck?" and "Did you see how deep the drop-off was on that mountain road?" and how we had to get out at various places and push the truck because of the conditions of the road. We didn't get to bed until after midnight, we were so busy rehashing the evening and hearing everyone's different version of what had happened.

We got up the next morning and put in another day of construction work. Cebien joined us for dinner that evening. As we were eating, suddenly the door opened and a Haitian entered, sweaty and out of breath. He went to Cebien and began talking to him. Cebien then relayed his message to us:

After we left the meeting in the field the night before, something wonderful had happened. This Haitian was so excited that he borrowed a bicycle and rode all night and all day to Cap Haitien to tell us the good news: Two witch doctors and their wives had turned to Christ!

As Americans we really didn't understand the significance of those conversions. We were told that very seldom does one hear of witch doctors being saved. If they do accept Christ and turn from their evil practices, their lives are threatened because other witch doctors put curses on them and attempt to kill them.

We were amazed that this Haitian would ride all night and all day just to tell us what had happened. He ate with us, stayed overnight, and rode back on his bicycle the next day. We came to call that unforgettable episode "The Trip to the Ends of the Earth," because we traveled that night to what did seem like the ends of the earth, and made it back safely, and two witch doctors and their families came to Christ. It was a life-changing event for us.

Today we are once again focusing on our work in the Dominican Republic as we wait for a stabilization of Haiti's political and social climate and watch what direction the university is going to take. Our prayer is that in the near future we will be working in Haiti again.

It is often only in retrospect that we, as humans, make sense of the series of events that make up our lives. Looking back, we are able to piece together the seemingly unconnected elements of our existence and discover the narrative thread that binds these elements together.

It all seems clear to me now.

It was 1992 and I was nine years old. My brother Jared and I were riding in the backseat of Jim and Mary Lou McDonald's black Cadillac playing the game "Name That Tune." The final song was a recording of "His Eye is on the Sparrow" played on the saxophone by Kim Costanza. My brother and I looked at one another with puzzled expressions. Jim could see that neither of us knew the name of the song, so he gave us a few hints. "His eye is on the...blank. It's a type of bird that starts with the letter 'S'." Having somewhat less than an exhaustive knowledge of either birds or Christian hymns, I yelled out the only thing I could think of:

"His eye is on the Sapsucker!" Indeed it was that day.

Two years later, I remember my father [Pastor Rick Crocker] bringing us together as a family to tell us that he, Jim, and a group from our church would be going on a short-term missions trip to Hato Mayor, Dominican Republic. I probably muttered something awful like, "Bring me back a t-shirt." We rarely understand the significance of events as they are occurring. If I had, I probably would have asked for two t-shirts.

Following that trip Jim and my father were never quite the same. In the years that followed, the Dominican Republic would find a place in my heart as I would establish long-lasting friendships with two young Dominicans who had come to live in Erie: Ricky Nolasco and Nelson Puello. Of course, at that point I had still never been to the island, nor did I know the role that it would play in my future.

Something happened rather unexpectedly on a Saturday in December of 1995. Jim, Ricky and I were riding four-wheelers through the snow on Jim's property. On this particular occasion, Jim was driving and I was seated behind him. All of a sudden, we took a sharp turn, and as we did we felt the four-wheeler starting to tip over. We were both tossed onto the cold, hard ground. The four-wheeler lay flipped on its side a few feet from us. Jim looked over to see if I was alright. From what he could tell, neither of us was badly hurt, so rather than offer any further consolation he said rather sternly,   "Don't tell your mother."

There would be a lot of things to come that I could never tell my mother — things I would see that I could never tell anyone.

As often happens with those whom we are close to in life, I lost contact with Jim, Ricky, and Nelson for many years. It would be a long time before those names would reclaim the significance they once held for me.

Ten years after Jim and I had crashed the four-wheeler, I was a senior at Nyack College, studying Spanish under the guidance of a professor from the Dominican. The professor and I got to talking about my post-graduation plans and she said, "It's good you studied Spanish. You may need it sometime in the future." I didn't think much of it at the time, but looking back, she may have been right.

In April of 2005, I received a phone call from Jim – completely out of the blue – saying that he was looking for someone to teach English at a university in Haiti, and that, if I was interested, he would fly me down to take a look at the school. I decided I would go for a visit – and the trip changed my life. I returned in August of that year, and stayed for two years.

While I was there I saw poverty the likes of which I had never before seen. In some areas of the country things were so bad that people were eating cookies made of dirt just to have something to fill their stomachs. I made some great friends in Haiti and have stories that even if I told you, you would never believe. Despite those great friendships, at the end of 2007 I decided to leave Haiti due to instability at the university.

I left feeling as if my time there had been a failure. I wasn't sure where to go, so I did what most people in my situation would do: I went home to live with my parents.

I felt so lost that year at home. Either God had grown silent or I wasn't listening. Then the phone rang. It wasn't God – it was Jim. He had another idea for me. To be honest, I was getting tired of Jim's ideas. He explained that he wanted me to go with him to the Dominican as an interpreter for three weeks. Somewhat hesitantly, I agreed to go. While I was there God spoke to my heart about the work being done there. I returned home knowing that God had something for me in the Dominican Republic.

As I write this, I have now worked at the Meeting God in Missions compound in the D.R. for more than a year. As a result, I've had the chance to reconnect with several old friends including Ricky and Nelson, and have made a number of new friends. One of those new friends is Kim Costanza, the saxophonist whose music was playing in Jim's car all those years ago. He now works as Meeting God in Missions' director of outreach, and has become one of my closest friends.

Something else happened this year. I recently got engaged to a girl who grew up in Hato Mayor. I often wonder if, during that first trip in 1994, perhaps my father and Jim drove past her as she played in the streets. Little would they have known what she would one day mean to me. Little would they have known that all these events would somehow come together as part of a divine story.

Over the course of the last 16 years, I have been blessed to be able to witness the extraordinary unfolding of God's story in the lives of ordinary believers in the United States, the Dominican Republic, and Haiti through Meeting God in Missions.

I now understand what God was trying to teach me at age nine as I rode in the back of Jim's car, and it is this: His eye is on the sparrow, and I know He's watching me.

Justin Crocker
Hato Mayor, 2009

6

LEADERS AND LEADINGS

Point Men

Even while we were ministering in Haiti, we continued to run multiple missions trips to the Dominican Republic each year. And from the late 90s until 2003, Henry Mercedes was our point man in the DR. He prepared all the sites, arranged housing for us, and was an all-around huge help.

But as time went on, Henry began to feel the call to become a pastor. In 2003, he decided to answer that call and he left MGM to become a pastor in Hato Mayor.

We then entered a time of transition, looking for God's next choice to fill Henry's role as Meeting God in Missions' representative in the Dominican Republic and assistant in everyday operations - a fairly important job as far as MGM was concerned.

For several months I prayed about the situation and tried to understand what God was going to do about it. I knew of only one or two English-speaking Dominicans who could conceivably help us. Was one of them God's choice, or was He going to bring somebody else along?

At the orphanage where we'd stayed before building our center, I had met a teenager named Arturo Betancourt. As I was praying, Arturo kept coming to my mind but by this time in 2003 he held a good position as an executive at the only factory in Hato Mayor. It seemed unlikely we could offer him enough money to compete with this factory, so I didn't dwell on that possibility very long.

But eventually I felt God was leading me to at least meet with Arturo. I had already talked to several people in Hato Mayor about him and they all said he was an exceptional young man, very honest, very talented, and a Christian. I also learned that he had a masters degree in computers which was very unusual. And to my surprise, more than one person mentioned that Arturo was interested in getting into Christian work. I began to think God might be directing us to contact this young man. We asked the Sunday School class and many MGM participants to pray, and we watched to see what God was going to do.

On our next trip to Hato Mayor, I went to Arturo's house. I sat down with him and explained our situation, and asked him if he might have any interest in joining with Meeting God in Mission. He said it was kind of ironic that I should ask, because he felt God had been speaking to him about leaving the factory and going into full time Christian work. I was excited to hear that he was looking for an opportunity to do just that. We agreed to pray about it, and he said he would come to the MGM center in two days at four o'clock in the afternoon and give me his decision.

We continued to pray, but no one else came to my mind. Two days later, four o'clock came and went as I waited for Arturo. Dinnertime arrived, and I sat down with the others to eat, disappointed because Arturo had not come. Suddenly an older man, a stranger, appeared at the door. He spoke with one of the cooks, who relayed his message to me: He was Arturo's father and he wanted to talk to me outside.

When I went outside, Arturo's father opened the back door of his car and there was Arturo, lying in the back seat. I looked in and saw that he had a cast on his leg.

Arturo told me what had happened. While he was out walking one night, praying about his decision and trying to discern what God wanted him to do, a passing motorcycle veered onto the sidewalk and hit him, breaking his leg. With a broken leg, he said, he had a lot of time to think and pray. And he felt God was calling him to quit his administrative position at the factory and come and join with Meeting God in Missions.

What a blessing for us! Arturo speaks fluent English. He is honest. He can do bookkeeping. He can sing and play music. He can also preach. So we ended up with a music director, a preacher, a bookkeeper and an honest Christian! He and his wife, Rosanny, joined Meeting God in Missions in December 2003 and have been a blessing to us ever since.

About that same time a family from Smethport, John Kio and his wife, Jenny, and three children, contacted me about the possibility of going down and staying in the Dominican Republic to work full-time as MGM missionaries. It was a foreign idea at first, far beyond anything we'd ever contemplated, and I wondered what God was trying to do.

We had several conversations, and they decided to come on a January 2004 mission trip. Throughout the rest of that winter and spring there was a lot of prayer and dialogue between the Kios and MGM. John Kio was a talented homebuilder who could build a house from the ground up, and we realized that he could be a great help to us in the DR, both in the maintenance and improvement of the MGM facility and in the construction of churches for the Dominicans and Haitians.

In the summer of 2004, John and his family moved down to the MGM center, committing themselves to the assignment for three years. During that time, John ran the facility, performed all the maintenance work, and made preparations for our construction jobs. He was an immense help to us.

It was difficult, however, for a family of five to live at the center. As a result, we purchased a piece of land adjacent to the center and between mission trips John began to build what is now called the Missionary House. For the next several years, trip participants helped John construct a beautiful home of approximately 3000 square feet, completing it around the end of 2006.

John and his family stayed in the DR for three years. In addition to their duties at the center, they also did evangelism work and John did some preaching. His children became very fluent in Spanish.

They had a little daughter who had a physical problem, and they had to bring her back and forth to the States several times for surgeries. Her condition was of great concern to them as well as to the MGMers. She was a beautiful little girl and we were all very concerned about her. When the Kios' three-year stint was up in 2007, they moved back to Coudersport and John returned to the construction business. We were grateful that God had brought us a multi-talented family who accomplished a great deal and was a blessing to many people.

In January of 2006, a group of people from Millcreek Community Church near Erie, Pa., led by Pastor Cyphers, came to Hato Mayor on a mission trip. Among them were Rob and Melissa Dunn. The whole group had a great time and when they got back home, Rob and Melissa came to talk to me, saying they had been praying for a number of years for an opportunity to go to the mission field and now they felt God was calling them to go to Hato Mayor to work as missionaries.

We had several lengthy discussions about Hato Mayor. By 2007, after they had been on a few mission trips, we all were convinced that God had called them to go to Hato Mayor and move into the missionary house the Kios had just vacated. So God, in His perfect timing, released the Kios and brought the Dunns into the life of Meeting God in Mission.

The two families differed in talents and interests. As I look back on it, God brought the Kios to help us in construction when we needed them; when the construction was concluded, their time was completed. Then the Dunns came, with gifts of serving and welcoming people. Rob can paint, weld, and do carpentry work, so they have helped finish and decorate the missionary house. Rob is in charge of running the facility as

John did before, and he does the maintenance on the property and vehicles. Both of these families have been a great blessing to MGM.

Most recently, Justin Crocker, son of my pastor Rick Crocker, came to Hato Mayor and began running a School of Ministry, preparing Dominicans and Haitians to preach in the sugar cane villages.

The Bus

In January of 2004, we conducted four one-week trips. Our numbers were growing by leaps and bounds, requiring us to hire multiple Dominican vehicles to transport the people to worksites, ministry areas, churches, etc. The cost to rent a truck in Hato Mayor had previously been $125 weekly, and we would need to rent a total of thirteen trucks for the January trips.

We did not realize that gasoline had almost doubled since we were there in 2003. In addition, every truck rental in Hato Mayor had joined to set a common price of one thousand dollars per week. In one year the charge per truck jumped from $125 a week to $1,000 a week. Suddenly it would cost $13,000 just to transport people to the places we needed to visit during the course of the trips.

Needless to say, that added around $9,000 to our projected costs and put a real strain on our budget. As a result, during that month in Hato Mayor I decided to investigate the possibility of purchasing a bus. Owning our own transportation in the DR would help our financial situation, and riding in a bus would be safer for our people than standing in the backs of open trucks, not to mention drier when it rained!

I came home in 2004 and started checking into buying a bus, but nothing worked out that whole year and our 2005 trips were confronted with the same situation again. I came home that year determined to look a little bit harder.

Other people also joined me in the search, and through the internet we discovered that about an hour and a half away in Butler, Pennsylvania, a large school bus sale was held annually. They generally had several hundred school buses available for purchase. The sale was coming up soon and bids were being taken, so another man and I went and looked at the buses, finding several that had potential for us.

I called Arturo, now our head man in the DR, and told him about the buses. That's when I learned that we could not bring a vehicle into the country that was older than five years. This was disheartening news, because we had spent two days checking out buses and I was preparing to go the next day and bid on one. All of them, however, were over ten years old. In fact, we'd learned that most school districts kept their buses until they were ten to fifteen years old. So we were right back where we'd been for over a year and a half.

We kept talking to people and searching the web, though, and eventually learned of one school district in the United States which sold buses that were five years and newer - Clymer, New York, only about 45 miles away. I called the school board, and they verified that every year they sold two five-year-old buses, because the contract on the transmission expired. (They'd had enough trouble with transmissions that they had decided it was more profitable to sell the buses at five years than pay for maintenance on them). They would receive bids throughout the month of June, and then the principal, the business manager and the head of bus maintenance would meet, open up the bids and sell the buses to the highest bidders.

I traveled to Clymer and looked at their buses. They were absolutely beautiful. I talked to a man there who, it turned out, was a Christian, and told him my problem: In June and July I was to be in the Dominican Republic and I wouldn't be able to attend the board meeting. He went to the school board on my behalf, and they moved the meeting for the bid openings to August.

That seemed an indication from God that we were on the right track, so we started praying that God would give us the wisdom needed to come up with a winning bid. We didn't really know what we were doing because none of us had ever been involved in anything like this before, so I got a copy of the winning bids for the ten buses sold over the last five years. Then we prayed and got our heads together and came up with bids for one school bus with 49,000 miles on it, and another with 72,000 on it.

I got the forms for the bids and filled them out. But on the morning we were to submit them, I had an uneasy feeling as I was praying, and so I sat down and figured a second bid for each of the buses. Then God seemed to tell me, "Why don't you ask him how many bids they are going to have, and if they say there are going to be a lot of bids, give them the high number. If there aren't going to be a lot of bids, give the low number."

So I took two bids, one in my right-hand pocket and one in my left-hand pocket. MGM board member Tim Pohl and I arrived at 11:30 a.m.; bids had to be in by 1:00 p.m. The man I'd talked with before came out to talk with us. He was a Christian and knew what we intended to use the buses for, and he wanted to see us get one.

"How many bids do you have?" I asked.

"The most bids we have ever had," he responded. That meant I had to go my right hand pocket and bring out the higher bid. So we submitted a bid for $17,600 for the bus with 72,000 miles on it.

We submitted the lower bid, $13,000, for the second bus, and I really thought God was going to give us a gift and we would get it for a lower bid. We went for lunch and returned at one o'clock. I asked if Tim and I could watch them open the bids, and they consented. There were about fourteen bids for the bus with the lowest mileage, and by the third bid we were out of the running, so we lost that bus.

When they opened the bids for the second bus, ours was third to the last. We won that bid by twenty-three dollars – and we won an absolute gift from God. This bus had tinted windows that would help us stand the tropical heat. It had an inside sound system and outside loudspeaker system. The sellers put brand new tires on it and filled it up with gas. It was an absolute, marvelous gift.

We brought that bus back to Erie and packed it to the rafters. Using it as a shipping crate, we filled it with all kinds of supplies for the missions work, then took our gift from God and sent it down to the Dominican Republic. It has been a gigantic blessing for us, saving us a lot of money and allowing people to ride inside in comfort and safety. We praise God for His gifts.

Ministry Teams and Leaders

Our earliest missions teams were small, comprised of perhaps twenty to thirty construction workers who went strictly for the purpose of building churches. God had brought along block layers Terry Young and his family and friends, and a young man named Jim Kibbe who, with his helpers, did carpentry work. It was a simple system: once the block walls were up, the block layers would help put up the trusses that Jim and his helpers had built. Then they put down tin for roofing, and the church was completed.

From the beginning of our first construction job, it was evident that Terry Young was a leader. Because he now owned a block laying company, he had a lot of experience. He also had a lot of general building knowledge and the workers naturally looked to him because of his expertise. We depended on him to tell us the sizes of windows and doors we needed, where they should be placed, and just about everything else in the beginning.

Terry Young became the construction leader for Meeting God in Mission and has served in that capacity ever since. He has been faithful through the 14-15 years that he has been with us. Terry's father Charlie (who recently died of cancer), Terry's son Adam, and his brother Kenny and nephews Clinton and Andrew have all been block layers for Meeting God in Mission. We are very grateful for their participation, because construction remains the backbone of many of the trips and all the construction starts with laying of blocks and footers.

As Terry has come in contact with a wide range of people through his work in northwestern Pennsylvania, he has freely spread the word about MGM mission trips. Many of those people have become interested in going. I can't begin to tell you how many people he has brought along on trips - carpenters and other block layers, laborers, cement finishers and home builders. Some of them have accepted Christ. So beyond Terry's construction knowledge, God has used him to bless many lives.

Jim Kibbe came on a mission trip soon after we got started, and he took over the carpentry end of Meeting God in Missions. He has been vital to MGM. Jim, with his carpentry crew, has designed and built trusses for the Haitian university, secondary schools, countless churches, and homes for pastors and other people. God has given Jim health and strength and has softened his heart on these mission trips. Like Terry, Jim has brought a lot of people on board - home builders, carpenters, and plain old laborers who hit nails or paint or put up tin or even climb atop church roofs in the hot sun with drill and screws to help put up the trusses. Jim certainly has been a blessing to Meeting God in Missions, filling a need that God has designed him to fill, and we are surely thankful for him.

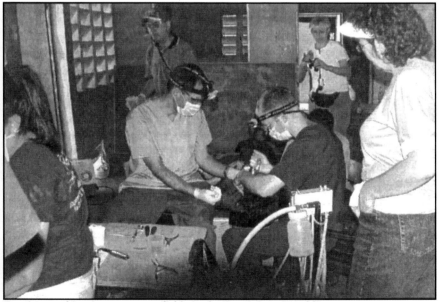

Dentists working in sugar cane fields in the Dominican Republic.

In the early days, when we were focused on construction, we never dreamed of running a vacation Bible school or offering the many other ministries we have now. But even then we often had a lot of Dominican kids running around the work sites, and sometimes the block layers would take turns going out and playing them. One worker in particular, Dean Jonas, loved to play with the children and teach them various games. We all got a lot of laughs watching him play in the dirt with those kids.

As time evolved and other people heard about what we were doing, people started coming on trips who really didn't have the skills to lay block or build trusses. I didn't recognize what was happening, but we were evolving. God was calling other people to join us because He had bigger plans. For instance, He was moving some construction workers to bring their wives so they could also have an experience with God. The next thing we knew, those wives, along with some others who came, started playing with the kids rather than doing construction work.

One year Rollie Fenton, from Greenville, Pennsylvania, brought his wife, Kitty, on a missions trip. Kitty was a worker and could labor right along with the men as we built our center in Hato Mayor. But we began to have a lot of difficulty with about fifteen boys who hung around the work area, watching the activity and hoping to get a sandwich when we ate. We couldn't keep them out of the way and were afraid they would get hurt, so it became my job to keep them away from the work site.

Finally, Kitty volunteered to quit working and take them aside to tell them Bible stories. Soon she was spending most of the day with those kids and we didn't see them much at all. She developed a relationship with them, and at the end of the week she had led every single one of the boys to Christ.

That is my recollection of the beginning of Vacation Bible School: Kitty leaving the work site to take some boys aside and lead them to Christ. It changed my way of thinking. We had focused on the construction of churches, but now God was showing me that building things was not what it was all about. Construction could give us the opportunity to share the gospel and lead people to Christ. And while we were leading Haitians and Dominicans to Christ, Americans were also meeting God in a new way and their hearts were being changed.

We now include Children's Ministry in every single trip, taking from fifteen to fifty children's workers each time. Many of these come from all over the United States as regulars on the children's ministry team. In their luggage are toys and gifts to give away to the children who attend Vacation Bible School. Some have been preparing skits, even forming groups which have practiced for several months in advance. They do all this so that when they come to the sugar cane villages, they are prepared to play with the kids, to share the gospel, and to give each one something to take home - perhaps a Jesus bracelet, a toy, an article of clothing or some type of game.

Often these workers split up and travel to two and three ministry sites a day, sharing the gospel with the children. I would estimate that at every Vacation Bible School site there are around 150 children, and sometimes as many as 50-75 parents who come along and sit on the perimeter, watching to see what happens. Moms and dads are included in the opening prayer time, after which they can watch as their kids participate in the children's activities. Parents are particularly welcomed on the last day when we share the gospel and invite people to accept Christ.

The Children's Ministry team leader is April Cush, a dance instructor from Ridgeway, Pennsylvania. She came on her first trip with a group from central Pennsylvania, intending to work construction When we got to the La Vega work site, however, we needed someone to do children's ministry. I'm not really sure how interested she was, but she sacrificed her plans and went to work with the children. Her life was changed forever, and she now goes on multiple trips every year for the sole purpose of leading the children's ministry.

In the DR, April has taught dance, developed skits and props, and written programs. (She has posted her material on a website, where children's ministry leaders can access her programs and day-to-day outlines for their own use). April holds an evangelistic program on the last day of each trip, giving kids and their parents the opportunity to accept Christ, and a number of people have accepted Jesus through the work of the children's ministry team.

It has been interesting to see April in action as she takes block layers and carpenters, in the afternoons when they have an hour or two off for rest, and puts them into Bible skits for the children. On the final day, with the emphasis on evangelism, they stop their construction work to become Moses or Daniel or another Biblical character, acting and speaking the part to help illustrate the gospel message.

God has put a desire in April's heart to serve these kids. We had gone several years without having a children's leader, so we're especially grateful that God has given her the gift of teaching and has put a burden on her heart to handle this responsibility for Meeting God in Missions.

My first experience with Meeting God in Missions came through one of the men in my church. He suggested Jim McDonald as a speaker at a men's retreat in west central Pennsylvania. Jim and I have often laughed about that retreat… it didn't go as well as planned!

However, I ended up in La Vega, DR, that year, along with several others from my church. What a great experience. Before the week was over, Jim and I sat down on a bench under a tree. With a legal pad and an ink pen, we outlined a plan to divide up the many responsibilities Jim was managing. We set up directors for various trip ministries and discussed

ways to allow MGM to incorporate others in strategic leadership roles.
Over the years we developed a handbook for trip leaders and job descriptions for ministry leaders. Each trip gave us an opportunity to experiment with ways to give Jim freedom to concentrate on his teaching. This deliberate effort to distribute leadership roles also allowed others to take ownership of their own ministry positions.

Meeting God in Missions is one of the few mission organizations that gives "short-termers" the opportunity to develop and execute their own ministry opportunities in the Dominican Republic. As a result, regulars come back yearly. The motto "Serving others on the island of Hispaniola" applies to the guests from up north as well as the residents of the DR. What a lesson that has been to me.   - Rev. Brad Preston

In 1997, Jim invited me along on a trip to the DR (this was the days before MGM had a name). That year I helped put a roof on Pastor Timan's church, the first roof Jim's group had ever built like that, and it survived Hurricane George in '98. So when we went back in January of 1999, I was called upon to help orchestrate roofing for about a dozen churches, each wanting a roof like Pastor Timan's.

Every workday morning for two weeks, two or three teams of workers would be dropped off in various Haitian villages located out in the sugar cane fields. We would work until the supplies ran out or the batteries went dead on our drills. Then we usually had time to play ball while waiting for the truck to come get us. Talk about being out of your comfort zone! There we were, out in the middle of nowhere without an interpreter - just the team, the villagers and God.

I guess I've become known as the person who organizes the MGM roofing projects. It's been a challenge, because that isn't my line of work. But in thirty-some trips we've roofed churches, schools and even some homes, and have been able to help a lot of people. I don't know exactly how many roofs we've put on, but it's always one or two a trip.

Over the years I've worked with many people and have been able to grab an idea from this one or that one to help make the job go easier. That continues to happen today on trips. It's still a challenge for me to get a plan together and get people working together, so it's always a plus to have a real carpenter to aid in getting the job done.

One year, as we loaded the truck with supplies before heading out to a village, I looked at the group that was boarding the vehicle. There were two other men besides myself, and a handful of ladies. I remember thinking to myself, How are we ever going to get this job done? But these people came prepared to work. We built the trusses, put them on the church, and put the purlins on, all in one day. That was one of the best groups I have ever worked with, so I've learned you can't always tell what's going to happen at the job site by who's there.

Besides, one of our favorite MGM sayings is, "It's not about the blocks"... or the roof or any other part of the projects. It's about the lives – Dominican, Haitian, and American - that are touched.

For instance, in Haiti I remember traveling to a church (the two-hour trip seemed to take us to the end of the earth and included getting stuck in a river bed). When we finally got to the end of the path, we had a church service and passed out Bibles. Afterward we returned to the place we were staying. When we got up for breakfast the next morning, we learned that a fellow had ridden his bike all night to come tell us that two witch doctors and one of their wives had been saved during that meeting. It was a serious thing for a witch doctor to become a Christian because it could mean life or death to him.

I've also seen many American lives touched as we worked beside each other all week. Grown men have come to me bawling like a baby, thanking me when I didn't know I'd done anything. I remember a young lady getting saved and saying it was because of how the men handled themselves at the job site.

There have been many good times over the years. I love to have fun and if we can keep laughing while we are working, it's always good. There have also been some trying times, and times of growth.

On a recent trip it seemed like it rained every day. Another fellow and I were talking about putting the tin on the roof, and I said we couldn't do it if it rained; it would be too slippery.

"We need to pray about it," he said, and we did.

The day we were to put the tin on the roof it rained all through devotions and breakfast. I was wondering where God was. We walked to the job site that day and by the time we were ready to put the tin on, the sun was shining on us. A hole appeared to open in the sky above us, although there were clouds all around the city. It seemed like the Lord was saying "O ye of little faith." God had to remind me once again that He's always there even when it doesn't seem like it.

I remember coming home from Edinboro Camp when I was six or seven and telling my parents that I was going to be a missionary, although I didn't really know what that meant. I forgot about it over the years and often felt like I probably missed my calling. I believe God has given me a second chance later in life through short-term missions. God's still working on me every trip I go on, whether it's teaching me patience through working with so many different personalities, or spending more time in the Scriptures and talking with him. One year I went my health wasn't the best and I had a bitter attitude. God really spoke to me, and He was able to break me. I found out later my wife had been praying for me.

I'm not the same person I was when I started going on MGM trips. Stepping out into the unknown has changed my life forever, and I would challenge everyone to take that step. I believe if you're open and willing God will use you... even if you don't think you can do anything.
      If you remember, I'm not a carpenter.
                                                            Jim Kibbe,
                                                            Erie, Pa.

I have been involved in teaching for years, but the time I have spent leading VBS in the Dominican has energized me like nothing else in my life. Only a few days into my first trip, I knew in my heart that I was to return and continue sharing God's love with the people of the DR. I have been on six trips thus far and would love to give you a collage of visuals that often go through my mind...
      ...a bench crammed with little bodies looking at me with big brown eyes, eagerly awaiting the lesson for the day...
      ...a street full of children, their "shields" held high, ready to fend off the ensuing attack of "evil" silly string...
      ...men sitting on a dirt floor with hands three times those of the little ones sitting next to them, helping to glue rhinestones onto a craft...
      ...being chased down the street by smiling faces and hearing "Hasta mañana!" ("Until tomorrow!") while riding away to the next VBS...
      ...offering the opportunity to have a personal relationship with the Lord and being surrounded by a group ready to accept the invitation to meet their Savior...
God has clearly used MGM as a way of showing me the gifts He has given me. My life has been enhanced by the opportunity to use those gifts, and by the people I have met. Some have become a supportive force in my life back in the States. (I love you, New Jersey!)
      One of the things I love about Jim is that when you get an idea and share it with him, he celebrates and cheers you on, offers some wisdom, and then lets you fly with it. And I cannot say enough positive things about his morning teaching sessions. The daily devotional times have been instrumental in my growth as a Christian.
      These trips have given me an opportunity to invite friends, students, and others from my church to join with me, and they've also allowed me

to share with many how God is moving in my life. I encourage anyone to say "yes" to going on a trip, where, I pray, your heart will be moved by the Lord through the hearts of the people of the Dominican Republic.

- April Cush
Kersey, PA.

7

FOLLOWING GOD INTO LA VEGA

In 1998 I was contacted by the Christian and Missionary Alliance in the Dominican Republic. They asked if we were willing to build a church in La Vega, a province in the central part of the country where they wanted to open up a work. They already had a pastor and some land he had obtained from the government; they only lacked a building. So we agreed to go to La Vega in March of 1999 and build them a church. Little did we know what that would entail and where our involvement would lead.

I noticed that our numbers were growing. Even after taking trips to Hato Mayor in January, there were forty to fifty people on the March trip to La Vega. The land for the proposed church was situated near a compound run by the Oriental Mission Society, and that is where we stayed. Although the OMS facility was aging, it was a large property with a swimming pool and it worked well for what I thought was going to be a one-time adventure. But at the conclusion of the week, we were asked to consider returning the next year to build a school beside the church.

We prayed about that for a while. I wasn't keen on going back, but the Americans had enjoyed themselves and were fired up about returning the following year. So the next year we did go back to La Vega and started the footer for a school. It was probably the hardest construction task we've encountered even to this day, because the footer for the two- or three-story building was to be three feet wide and four feet deep, and our tools were picks and shovels.

It was, in fact, strictly pick-and-shovel through a garbage pile. Drug users had frequented the site and there were needles all over the place. We dug through bricks and blocks and rocks and clay and we all earned our money that week.

The Water Tower Church

Four of us stayed over an extra week to try to finish up the footer (the school was later completed and is in operation), and by the last night we were exhausted. We had finished digging, had eaten supper, and were lying down when a knock was heard at the door. It was the head missionary of the DR's Christian and Missionary Alliance.

He wanted us to accompany him to a church service being held that evening about forty-five minutes away, near Moca, because the pastor there wanted to meet and talk with us. I said, "I'm not going to go. I'm too tired." The other three men agreed to go. As they were getting dressed, I thought, *Well I had better go because I am going to miss something if I don't.* So all four of us went with the missionary.

We drove far into the country, to a place with several houses and a tiny store. We parked and I looked for the church, but saw nothing until the missionary told us that church was held in a one-car garage. We went over to the garage and saw three pews, each seating maybe four or five people, and a little sound system at one end with a tiny speaker on the wall.

After the service we were eager to leave because early the next morning we were heading back to the States. First, though, the pastor had a story to tell.

She informed us that a gentleman seated toward the back of the garage church that evening had, fifty-one years earlier, built a water tower for this community. He had been commissioned to do this by a very wealthy man who owned most of the land in that part of the country and needed a watering place for his livestock.

The builder of the water tower was at that time the only Christian in that part of the Dominican Republic. After he finished constructing it, he took a knife, as the story went, and carved a prophetic message in Spanish in the side of the water tower: God would send somebody by the year 2000 to build a church on that property.

The missionary who'd brought us was somewhat skeptical of the story, so we all crossed the street, climbed over a barbed-wire fence, waded through briars... and there, lo and behold, was an old water tower that had been built in 1949. As we walked around it, the missionary spied something carved in the wood. Soon he was spitting on it, wiping it clean with the sleeve of his white dress shirt, and translating the inscription: God will bring somebody to build a church on this land before 2000.

And this was 1999.

We were dumbfounded. Then Ernie Kalgren, one of our workers, elbowed me in the ribs and said, "You know, I think God is telling us something."

"I don't think he is telling us anything," I replied. I was trying to think of reasons why we couldn't come out there and build a church.

I asked the pastor, "Where was the church supposed to be built?" She indicated a plot of ground approximately two acres in size and surrounded by a barbed wire fence. As she pointed it out, we put a light on it. The only thing inside that fence was the water tower and an old broken-down basketball hoop. All the Americans started laughing then, because I had been a former basketball coach. It surely seemed that not only was God indicating exactly where the church was to be built, He was bringing a basketball coach there to see that it got done.

So although we'd intended to make only one trip to La Vega, we returned the next year and built a church beside the water tower. Because of the unique story behind the project, about eighty people came on that second trip - easily our biggest group up to that time.

And every year we go back there. The plot of ground is now mowed and the church is surrounded by a white picket fence. The lady pastor had a backdrop built behind the pulpit area and had the trusses painted white – which looked so beautiful that we've painted the trusses in every one of the dozens of Dominican churches we've built since then. The church is very elegant in style and they are growing by leaps and bounds. They've even cut a hole in the side of the metal tower and inside, in their "Jordan River," they now hold baptismal services. We've been blessed as we've seen how God has blessed them.

During that second trip to La Vega, I had nine requests from pastors who were holding services in fields or in a home or out on the street, and wanted churches built. We started investigating and praying, and the next thing we knew we were regularly coming back to La Vega. We can't keep up with all the requests. It has been one of the most exciting adventures that we have had with Meeting God in Missions – not only because we've now built over a dozen churches around La Vega, but because the Holy Spirit has come in power on three or four of these trips, prompting confession of sins and changing lives. These trips have been a blessing to a lot of people.

A gentleman from New Jersey by the name of John Lowry has become very involved with Meeting God in Missions. He's been a kind of "recruiter" for MGM in his home state, and the number of New Jersey participants increases every year. At first they only came to La Vega, but now they also come on trips to Hato Mayor. They've created their own website for Meeting God in Mission New Jersey, and their own recruiting system throughout their state. As a result, well over one hundred people, perhaps closer to two hundred, from New Jersey now accompany MGM trips to Hato Mayor and La Vega.

Soon after building the water tower church, we were requested to build a church in Santiago, a town near La Vega. It would be the largest one we had ever built - over eighty feet long and approximately thirty-six feet wide. We agreed, and went and completed the church the following year. It was a major undertaking for us, but it's been amazing to watch that church grow. They have built Sunday school rooms onto the back of the church and attendance probably tops six hundred by now, including perhaps one hundred and fifty youth. We have been there and it is standing room only. It's now one of the biggest churches in the Dominican Republic and growing by leaps and bounds.

La Vega Haitians

During our time in La Vega, we kept hearing about Haitians who were walking from Haiti to La Vega – a distance of approximately one hundred miles just from the border. They were looking for work and sleeping on the ground. We kept running into some of these people as we were visiting churches. In fact, while constructing a church at La Vega our second year we also we built a Haitian church on the side of a mud hill.

It was an interesting experience. About seventy of us set out for the site. When we couldn't drive any farther, we walked up the side of the mountain. About half to three-quarters of a mile up the mountain, we spied a hut sitting about forty feet up in the air on the side of a mud hill. It was a Haitian church, constructed of tin, with palm leaves on the roof.

We followed a dirt path which led around the hill and up to the church, and took turns looking at the little structure, which seated twelve Americans. The trusses were made from five-foot tree limbs, so when we stood, our heads were above the trusses. A string of Christmas tree lights, plugged into an extension cord from a house next door, provided the only illumination for the evening services.

Many of the Americans sat outside on the mud hillside and cried. The Haitians showed up while we were there and we held a church service together, some of us inside and some out. The following year we came back and built them a church, digging out the hillside to make it fairly level with the road. Their new building seats approximately two hundred. Our Vacation Bible School is big there, with two to three hundred neighborhood children attending. It's been an exciting adventure.

Hector's Church

During that time, we met a variety of Haitian pastors who were trying to minister to their people while holding church services in all different kinds of places. One of them was a man named Hector.

Hector seemed to be the most organized of these pastors. He had a plan, in writing, for organizing all the Haitians and Haitian pastors in La Vega, Santiago, and the surrounding area. We had several meetings with Hector, and he kept telling us he needed a church and a place for the Haitian men to be able to sleep up off the ground. Every year, in fact, Hector would bring a proposal.

Sometime around 2004-2005 a group of us sat down and talked about Hector's plan. After praying about it, we decided to look for land.

The land where Hector wanted to locate was incredibly high-priced, so we looked elsewhere and found two sites for sale - one a gorgeous piece of level land, and the other on the side of a hill so steep you could hardly build anything on it. So we went back and looked at the first property, prayed, and decided we would buy it.

Five or six people stood with me as we prayed over the land and asked God to provide the resources to buy the property, which was priced at $25,000. As we returned to the car, a couple from Greenville, Pennsylvania, said they were very pleased with that land and that this project was really on their heart.

I said, "Well, you know we are going to have to pray hard that God will show us where the money is going to come from and that we'll be able to raise the $25,000."

They said, "No, it's only $20,000."

I said, "No, no, no, we talked to the pastor and the lawyer and he talked to the owner, who said he would sell it for $25,000."

They replied, "No, it's only $20,000."

"Well, how did you get $20,000?"

"We are going to give you $5,000. We'll promise that amount right now."

So before we even got in the car, God had provided $5,000 for us. Amazingly, within two months God had provided the other $20,000 to buy the land.

By the time we came back the following year, the land had been purchased and put in Meeting God in Missions' name. The Haitians in the area were very excited and eager to help build their church and had already dug the footer in preparation for the construction. We sent a smaller group one week early who, together with the Haitians, poured the footer and the floor and had an exciting time in the process.

God provided plumbers, labors, cement finishers and block layers needed for the project. At the end of our two weeks, the church was completed by the largest group that had ever gone on a mission trip with Meeting God in Mission. Just over one hundred people, about sixty of them from New Jersey, came to work on this project.

Meanwhile, following our purchase of the land the previous year, the Haitians had erected a tree limb church. It had walls of chicken wire braced by tree limbs, and a roof of limbs covered with palm leaves. This is where they had held services for a year. When we came to build the church, we used the tiny tree limb structure for Vacation Bible School. So our team of about one hundred people was divided between Vacation Bible School, laying blocks, painting, and general labor.

It was a busy scene. The sixth day of the second week found us putting the peaks up, installing the trusses, and working inside and outside to get it finished. (This was a larger church, with a three-bedroom apartment for the pastor and his large family). At one point I counted over sixty workers, including block layers, people putting up the trusses and laying the tin on the roof, painters working inside and out, plumbers finishing on the inside, and even workers installing windows in the walls as we were painting. It was a sight to behold.

On the seventh and last day, we finished painting, cleaned everything up, scrubbed the floors down, installed the front door, and held a church service that evening at seven o'clock. We had over one hundred Americans and about two hundred and fifty Haitians in attendance. Over one hundred people stood outside the church; the rest were packed inside. The church service lasted a little over two hours. Someone spoke in English, which was interpreted into Creole and from Creole to Spanish. It was exciting to worship in the new church along with several hundred people in three different languages.

At the end of the service, there was an altar call and several people were saved. And then another amazing thing happened. The Haitians wanted to sing.

At the beginning of the service, Hector had approached me and asked if I thought it would be alright if they sang in their church. I said, "Pastor, you're in charge of this church. It now belongs to you and your congregation. You can sing, you can dance, you can do whatever you want to do. This is your church." So after the benediction the Haitians had a celebration! They all stood up and started cheering, because they now realized this was their church and they could worship God in whatever way they desired.

The Haitian men began singing and dancing across the front of the church. We stood up on the benches to watch as they sang and sang, playing guitars and keyboards and dancing up a sweat in that sweltering tropical heat. Then we had a time of prayer and concluded an unforgettable night.

The next year we returned to build another structure on that property – the housing facility to provide Haitian men shelter from the weather and a place to sleep. Jeff Holes, the architect with MGM who had designed the church, also designed these living quarters. This large building, which would sleep sixty-five Haitian men, included shower and restroom facilities, a dining room, and a kitchen.

It was our plan to complete the construction by the end of the week. To meet that goal, we knew we would need sixty-five metal beds with mattresses. So Arturo went to La Vega in advance and found someone to make the beds for us, and also went down to Santo Domingo and purchased the mattresses.

God had provided lights and fans through a sale at Lowe's. We paid a quarter of their usual price, and were able to bring down all the fans and lighting for the church and the housing facility at a fraction of what we'd have normally paid in the United States or in the DR.

We built a cooking area and bought a refrigerator for the kitchen. Thankfully, MGMer Rich Graden was able to do tile work, and we installed tile countertops. We also used the talents of plumbers, electricians, carpenters, block layers and laborers - a wide range of people numbering over one hundred. At the end of six days of work, the facility was completed and we dedicated it on the seventh day before leaving.

The church (with pastor's apartment) and housing facility together cost over one hundred thousand dollars. God was faithful. Money came in from a variety of sources, including people I'd never met who had learned what we were doing and wanted to be a part of it.

As a result, these Haitians have a beautiful compound with its own well and septic system, making it self-sufficient. Haitian men now live there. In order to stay at the compound, these men must be Christians and attend church services in the evenings and on Sunday. They need to follow certain rules of behavior and share responsibilities in cooking and cleaning. They pay a little bit for food, but beyond that we take care of all the other expenses.

Each year we take in a few more men, working towards our goal of having sixty-five men sleeping there and worshipping God together.

The church, now Christian and Missionary Alliance, has been very, very successful and has a large attendance. Needless to say, Hector is elated over what has been happening. Where it will all lead, I don't know, but I'm convinced God is behind this. He has provided all the resources so far, and He'll continue to lead the way.

The Santiago Church

By this point we had built eight churches in La Vega, along with the housing facility for Haitians. And to this day we receive numerous requests each year from people who need churches. It appears that God is going to continue our March trips to La Vega for many years to come, in response to these never-ending requests from pastors and other Christians who need help in some way.

In 2007 we received a rather unusual proposal from a pastor who even brought a blueprint of the church God had laid upon his heart. I looked at the blueprint and told him, "You know, this church is way bigger than anything we've ever tried to build. It is two stories with a balcony and looks like it could seat hundreds."

As we talked, he began to tell me the story of how he got the land. He said he pastored a little church that was located on the edge of the camp where we were staying. The church had been there a number of years. Recently, however, it became necessary for them to put the church into someone's name, so they chose one of the deacons. This man later decided to sell the church out from underneath them and gave them a year to find another place to worship.

The mayor of La Vega heard about the situation. The town was building a beautiful subdivision about a mile and a half from where we were staying, and the mayor told the pastor that the congregation would be given a large corner lot, one of the nicest in the whole subdivision, if they could start a church within a year. If they didn't start a church, the lot would be used for another purpose.

I had never met this pastor before. I didn't know his congregation. But he joined me the next morning and together we drove the four or five blocks to this gorgeous subdivision. The paved road had curbs and street lights. There were already a few houses built, with a few more under construction - all big, beautiful homes. I thought, Boy oh boy, how did you get this land? He showed me the plot the mayor was offering. It was perfectly level, with enough space for four churches.

As we looked at the property, I told him what we could do for him. The largest church we had ever built was eighty-some feet long. We would do the same for him, and make it about thirty-eight feet wide. To fit the neighborhood, we would go the extra mile and do something special, making it more elegant by adding a front porch with a little balcony and a sidewalk out to the road.   The pastor was quite excited about that.

We went home and designed the church.   The next year we came back and started construction, working to meet the mayor's deadline. A young lady named Pam Mayle accompanied us.   Pam had created a beautiful stained glass window for the MGM center in Hato Mayor as her contribution to God and to missions.   After our last trip to La Vega, I had talked to her about putting a stained glass window in this church.   She was excited about the idea, and she, along with several other people, spent most of a year developing the window.   My wife, Mary Lou, who is an artist, agreed to help paint the stained glass.

With the stained glass all ready, we returned to La Vega to construct the church.   Our numbers continued to grow; we took 120-125 people on this trip.   Much pre-construction work had already taken place.   In addition, the fabrication of the stained glass window, the building of trusses, and the construction of benches took place off-site at our compound.   We built the most – and largest - pews for a church that we'd ever done.

One of the week's highlights came when we joined with the congregation, which was now meeting on the balcony of a house.   I hadn't realized that all of the workers at the camp where we stayed - our friends for the past several years - attended this church.   They had never said a word to me, never asked for anything.   Now it was exciting to realize that we were building a church for all these friends.

The Dominicans did the finishing touches while we were building the walls, and at the end of the week we held a dedication service.   The facility was absolutely spectacular.   The floor had been poured.   The stained glass window was installed.   The front porch was constructed. The sidewalk was laid.   It truly was a gorgeous church that seated three to four hundred people.   And God had provided eighty thousand dollars for the project.   Next year we are going to go back and paint it, and then the church will be totally completed.   I believe the Dominicans also plan to add Sunday School classrooms and bathrooms.

No End in Sight

From 1998 to the present, God brought many American pastors on the La Vega mission trips, many more than came to Hato Mayor.   It's a trend that just started and kept growing.   Because of the large number of participants, we had to split up and go to two or three churches a night. That meant we needed several pastors each night to do the preaching, so we made good use of the six or seven pastors now accompanying us.

Rob Douglas, from Greenville, Pa., was one of those pastors.   Rob came to me around 2004 or 2005 and asked if I needed help running a trip.

I said, "I certainly would appreciate that." He became the first pastor to run a trip, and it was to La Vega.

God used Rob to change the whole profile of Meeting God in Missions. Now a pastor leads every trip we take anywhere. We are running ten to twelve trips annually and have probably fifteen to twenty pastors traveling with us over the course of the year. Each pastor preaches two to three times a week.

We also started training sessions for Dominican pastors. Several American pastors go down on their own throughout the year and hold week-long conferences, teaching Dominican pastors (who have never had any training) how to run a church, how to prepare a sermon, and how to do many other things. The involvement of the pastors has been a real blessing to Meeting God in Missions and to the Dominicans and Haitians as well.

In La Vega we're now building multiple churches per trip. In 2008, we actually constructed three different facilities: a small church, a large church, and an addition on an orphanage for homeless kids.

That year, instead of taking the last day off to go to the beach as our workers normally do, the MGMers pooled their own money and built an addition on the orphanage. They had a little picnic when it was finished, and it was an exciting time. We built a small church for another lady who had been holding services out in the middle of the street. She was grateful and many people were blessed at that construction site.

We are now consistently taking around one hundred and twenty people to La Vega, which allows us to run two and three Vacation Bible School sites in the morning and three or four additional VBS sites in the afternoon, as well as work on several construction projects. It is exciting to see two sets of trusses being built, two sets of benches being built, and two Vacation Bible Schools going on, and then each evening divide up and attend three different church services. In addition, we hold a week-long pastor's conference on each trip with anywhere from thirty to fifty Dominican pastors coming for three hours in the evening to be trained by American pastors who want to honor God and help His church.

Where all this is going to end I certainly don't know, but the La Vega adventure has truly been exciting.

_____

Here in Soto, La Vega, the Haitians didn't have a place to meet and worship the Lord. MGM helped us buy a property and build a church where the people could meet, and also a dorm for those without a place to sleep. We feel supported and encouraged by this ministry that God has brought to our country to come alongside and help us. Arturo and his family have helped to strengthen us as well.

Our school is going very well. The teachers are encouraged by the contributions we have received. Around us we see many little Haitians needing education and we are concerned that tomorrow they don't become delinquents who are a problem for the country. We are praying for them to be able to come to school. Most lack transportation or their relatives are very poor. Our passion is to have a center for these kids in Soto.

- Hector Julio Cedeno,
Pastor of Christian Church in Soto, La Vega

We all need time-outs. They serve a purpose, whether it's a child put in a corner, a team huddled to regroup, or a believer needing moments with God. It is allotted time to focus on a specific goal, or to restore or strengthen our inner being.

That is how I look at Meeting God in Missions. On my numerous trips with MGM, God has used me as a construction helper, a cook, a singer, a medical assistant, a stained glass window fabricator, etc. Those jobs were not the primary reason I was there, but they were the vehicle that God used to bring me to my "time-outs," where He revealed His will for my life, helped me to be obedient to his callings, and helped me grow in my walk.

My time-outs in the D.R. and Haiti got me off the hamster wheel of busyness for a few days in order that God could have my full attention to help me focus, to bring spiritual restoration, to confer with godly leaders and spirit-filled friends, and to regroup and center myself in God's game plan.

MGM trips are where visions are revealed and dreams are born, but you wonder if they will survive once back home. For instance, during a quiet time on one of those MGM trips I was reading The Dream Giver by Bruce Wilkinson. I shared with my friends that I felt God calling me into a different career that I felt was more of a ministry than a job. I knew it would mean sacrifices, not only on my part but on my family's and I wondered, even doubted, if God could ever make it happen.

But it's when friends encourage you and God arms you for His purposes that you return home with a new confidence in your spiritual walk and in what God can do through you if you are obedient. I am happy to say that six years later, through obedience and perseverance, that God-given dream has been fulfilled...and it all started in a time-out with God.

I have learned from my trips with MGM that God works and fulfills his purpose through ordinary people, whether it be building a church, birthing an eyeglass ministry, starting a revival in a school, or changing a career. And it can all start with a whisper in a time-out....

- Pamela Mayle,
Erie, Pennsylvania

8

A BLESSED PARTNERSHIP

In 2003 a girl named Allie Myers made her first trip to the DR. She was so impacted by the experience that upon her return to Ohio she talked with the headmaster of Cuyahoga Valley Christian Academy (CVCA) where she attended. Because CVCA offered a yearly mission trip to upperclassmen, she wondered if her class could go to the Dominican Republic.

Because the school planned to send the students to Haiti, Mr. Halley had no interest at that time. But by the next year many parents were not happy with their children going to such a volatile country. So in 2004 Mr. Halley took sixteen students on an MGM trip to the DR, where they had a transforming week.

In 2005, half of the class went to Hato Mayor and half to Haiti. Then in 2006 the entire group made the week-long trip to Hato Mayor and were deeply spiritually moved. CVCA has sent their students every summer since, and in 2010 there will be an alumni trip as well as a class trip, with about 125 attending.

But it's not about the statistics; it's about what God has done in hearts and lives - and He's not finished yet. He continues to meet and transform students, parents, and faculty through these yearly trips.

Read on... I'll let them tell you about it in their own words...

CVCA's 2008-2009 Year-end Report

(Cover page excerpt)

Dear Friends:

The 2008-2009 school year was one of the most remarkable years in the history of CVCA. In the wake of an unusual moving of God among CVCA's senior class as they served in the Dominican Republic in June 2008, they returned to school to provide a level of spiritual leadership rarely witnessed in a high school setting.

The consistent witness of the class of 2009 set a remarkable tone for a school year, which saw our students learn, perform, compete, achieve and serve at the highest levels. From musical and theatre performances, to competing at the state and/or national level in athletics, FBLA, and Forensics, to preparing 108,000 meals to be sent to Third World countries through the Feed My Starving Children program, CVCA students invested their gifts and talents in countless Christ-honoring ways. As dedicated faculty, staff, and families walked alongside our students throughout the year, CVCA made great strides in its aim to be a community that trains and mentors and a community of authentic faith...

Roger Taylor, Ph.D.
President

Kyle Gerycz, CVCA graduate:
         In 2008 God blessed me with the greatest week of my life, when I came on the CVCA trip to the DR with Meeting God in Missions. Besides being with some of the poorest people in the world, I was able to see my own group truly have an experience with God.
         Partway through the week I told my friend, "Whatever verse I see first will be my verse to focus on today." The Bible fell open and I saw Romans 8:5: "Those who live according to the sinful nature have their minds set on what that nature desires. But those who live in accordance with the spirit have their minds set on what the spirit desires" (NIV). That night I talked to Jim about my addiction to pornography. I recommitted myself to Christ and was made new. Instead of trying to fix my problem on my own, I gave the Spirit control to fix it for me.

The last day of our trip was share night. People talked about how they were thankful to come down and see some of the poorest people in the world on fire for God, and they said they wouldn't take things for granted anymore. But I knew this trip was about more than just seeing poor people; it was about having an experience with God. So with the help of the Holy Spirit talking through me, I told my story and how the night before, God had set me free.

The next thing I knew, everyone was crying and telling of their own addictions and problems. They were surrendering their lives to God as well. We came back a totally different class, out to change our school. The Holy Spirit worked miracles at our school and in the lives of those around us, including parents and friends. I love MGM and Jim McDonald, but above all I praise the Holy Spirit every day for truly setting me free.

Gail Gerycz, mother of Kyle (above):

Kyle gave me full permission to share the following in hopes that others may find the forgiveness and healing power that only comes through a relationship with Jesus Christ...

Background

For ten days between their junior and senior year of high school, CVCA offers an overseas mission trip opportunity through MGM. When Kyle's class departed for the DR, Greg and I prayed that they would be "emptied of self and filled with the power of the Holy Spirit through Christ Jesus." Little did we know how God planned to do just that.

Nine days later, we met the returning group. How was the trip? "Awesome" seemed to be the word of the day. When we asked Kyle to tell us about it, he handed us a notebook and asked us to read it first. So Greg and I sat down together and began to read Kyle's journal.

The Journal

Days 1-3. Kyle wrote about trips to the Haitian villages in the Dominican sugar cane fields, working with the children at the Compassion International school, and about the times of worship and teaching at the MGM center. The group was learning that God wants all of their heart. They were taught about the power of the Spirit living in them, and were challenged to give control of their lives over to God.

Day 4. Kyle described the evening with one word: "change." He said he would never be the same after he and a classmate spent some time talking to Jim. He then shared his struggles with a friend and asked him to help hold him accountable.

Day 5. Kyle found his life verse: "Those who live according to the sinful nature have their minds set on what that natures desires; but those who live in accordance with the Spirit have their minds set on what the Spirit desires" (Rom. 8:5 NIV). But Greg and I were totally caught off-guard by what we read next. Kyle wrote that pornography had kept him from a deep relationship with the Lord. Greg and I were aware that years ago Kyle had twice encountered computer pornography, but we had no idea the stronghold those incidents had on Kyle. Our son had been carrying that burden on his own until finally going to Jim McDonald. Jim encouraged Kyle with truths from God's Word and Kyle found God's forgiveness, making a definite choice to give the Lord complete control over his life and live by the Spirit. It was an "aha" moment in his journey with Christ. Jim also told Kyle that the Lord might sometime prompt him to share his story in order to help others.

That evening the entire group went into a sugar cane village and showed the Jesus film. Through an interpreter, Kyle had the privilege to share with one of the Haitians how to accept Christ. "This was an amazing day!" he wrote. Indeed, it must have been.

Day 6. They shopped in Santo Domingo, where the market streets were filled with paintings of naked bodies. Pornography was right in Kyle's face, yet he wrote that it had "zero affect on me. The Holy Spirit filled my heart to block out Satan." It was a day of overcoming through the power of the Spirit. That night, Kyle shared his story with some of the guys who he thought may have a similar struggle. It felt like God spoke through him in a way that was helpful to the other guys.

Day 8 (last day): The journal entry began: "UNBELIEVABLE!!" That evening, the entire group met in the "Upper Room, " MGM's worship center. As Kyle listened to others voicing observations and experiences from the week, he knew God wanted him to share his also. So after leading in prayer, Kyle shared his struggle with the effects of those brief experiences with pornography. He testified to the amazing power of the Holy Spirit that week, and asked someone to read Romans 8:1-5.

Afterward, friends surrounded him and prayed for him, and people he didn't know came up to support him or to ask how to have what he now had. Jim, Kyle, and others shared Scripture with those needing release from the bondage of sin. Students recommitted themselves to Christ and to each other.

In the process, walls came down and the class united in a way that Jim and the CVCA leaders had never witnessed. The students realized that this newfound love must spread in their school. They needed to help the underclassmen fall in love with Jesus, stop hiding behind a "Christian" façade, and seek the power of the Holy Spirit to keep them from sin. They prayed and left the Dominican eager to help their school when it opened that fall.

    Kyle had thought he was simply being obedient to the Spirit by sharing, just taking one more step toward being free from the bondage of pornography. Yet God had a bigger plan, a plan to bring glory to Himself. The entire class, along with teachers, administrators and other chaperones, were brought into a deeper relationship with Jesus Christ that night. This group returned home changed.

Back Home

    The senior class grew closer to Christ and each other throughout the remainder of the summer. Here's just some of what we've been blessed to observe since that time…

- Kyle continues to have a morning quiet time to this day . Throughout the past year, he has read through many books of the Bible and recorded the insights he's received. He earned a full academic scholarship to a top engineering university, where he plans to pursue a degree in engineering, hoping to one day expand the *Meeting God In Missions* concept.
- The students organized a special welcome for the underclassmen on the first day of school. The seniors wore hot pink shirts bearing their name and a message on the back encouraging underclassmen to ask them for anything – a hug, a word of encouragement, directions, prayer, etc.
- The CVCA administration granted the students' request to hold a time of worship each Monday before school, in which teachers, administrators and underclassmen join together as seniors lead the worship. This continues today!
- Throughout the school year, members of the senior class organized various outreach opportunities, including raising over $17,000 for 100,000 meals for the organization *Feed My Starving Children.*

    This testimony is an example of the scriptural truth: *obedience brings blessing!* Committed obedience to Jesus Christ has resulted in uncounted blessings in many, many lives. Praise be to our Lord and Savior!

Greg Hojnacki, CVCA graduate:

    On the 2008 trip to the DR, I led worship with my friend, Andy Hoffman. The second night, as we were playing guitar in the Upper Room, people started coming up one by one. Soon we began experiencing the most intense worship I have ever been a part of. Afterward we gathered - a pile of sweaty, crying, broken people - to rededicate our lives to God. I was on my knees crying out to God for forgiveness because I knew the life I had lived for the past seventeen years was completely wrong and I was tired of being an immobile Christian.

The next night a similar thing happened, and as we continued throughout the week, our class bonded more and more. At the end of the week, we made it our mission to go back to the United States to change our school and to impact the world around us.

When school started, we challenged ourselves to meet every single Monday morning at 7 a.m. for a time of worship and prayer. It started off with just older students, but then faculty began coming, and also kids from seventh grade all the way up to the seniors. Some of them we never expected to see there. Lives began to change in front of our eyes.

Many faculty had been impacted as well on that MGM trip. God had created an amazing atmosphere of love and understanding between the teachers and ourselves, until now I could sit down and pray with teachers whenever I wanted, which I'd never felt comfortable doing before.

If it weren't for this missions trip, my life might have never been changed. I have learned to step out of my comfort zone and sell out for Jesus Christ. I am going into college knowing I am saved through the blood of Christ and understanding that I can make a difference in the world by example, and that is what I plan to do.

Maggie Hess, CVCA graduate:
I grew up in a good Christian home, yet I carried many burdens that I didn't think God could take away from me. But on this trip, God showed up in my life. After worship one night, my classmates and I gave our lives completely over to God. He delivered me from all those burdens and my relationship with Him became real.

Part of the class had been supposed to go to Haiti and the rest were to come to Meeting God in Missions. But because of political conditions in Haiti, we all came to the Dominican Republic - which was a God thing because we were together and He showed up and unified our divided class, and kindled a flame in us.

We brought that flame back to the other students in the school and to the teachers and administration. People saw the difference in us. Families didn't know what happened to their kids because we were loving God and each other, doing quiet times, and just acting differently. Jim was getting calls from parents asking, "What happened to our kids? What happened?" I guess he just had to tell them that God showed up and our relationship with Him became real and now we were living how we should live.

I still carry a mental picture of a couple kids singing and another kid with his guitar and the remaining one hundred kids on our knees crying out to God and rededicating our lives to Him. In fact, that MGM trip has become a memory stone for us. When we look back on it we are reminded to live our lives for God and God alone. Now we are going off to college knowing how to live as Christians in love with God.

Daniel Richards, CVCA graduate:

The 2008 trip to the Dominican Republic changed my life forever.

The second night, while some were worshipping in the upper room, others of us were still downstairs and we missed the awesome time of repentance and worship. I was really disappointed. Then when I went to share my disappointment with a friend, a prayer meeting broke out in the room I'd just left – and I missed that too!

Greg Hojnacki found me with my head under my pillow, crying and praying, and he asked me, "What are you crying about? What do you want?"

I said, "I want God."

He said, "Well, if you want Him, just take Him." So that was the first night I really took hold of what God had to offer. The rest of the week was just an amazing experience. I have never felt that much camaraderie between our class.

Jim challenged us to welcome everyone on the first day back to school that fall. Many CVCA soccer players, myself included, were on that trip, and we wanted to do something different for the soccer season. We don't play any Christian teams, so we decided that after each game we would pray with a player from the other on the team if we felt God leading us to do that. It took us thirty seconds to pray with the person, but the way God worked through that simple action was one of the most amazing things about the school year. Some didn't know what praying was; others were saying, "Thank you so much for praying with me." Throughout the season we heard stories about people talking about our prayer initiative, and one of the local churches even did a sermon on it. I think God really used us to share who He was through that.

Shelby Mitchell, CVCA graduate:

Something felt special about this trip, even when I first landed at the airport in the Dominican Republic. I knew the experience would impact me and I figured, "Oh, I will connect with a little kid here and it will be so awesome"...

... but I connected with God.

On the second night we were worshipping together upstairs, and all of a sudden people just started praying, pouring out their hearts to God. I never heard such deep prayers spoken out loud to God. It really moved me, and I cried out to Him, too, putting it all out on the table and giving

Him every single ounce of me for the first time in my life.

Later I went to my Bible and opened it straight to Psalm 69: "Save me, Oh God, for the flood waters are up to my neck. Deeper and deeper I sink... I am exhausted from crying for help. My throat is parched and dry. My eyes are swollen with weeping, waiting for my God to help me... But I keep right on praying to you, Lord, hoping this is the time you will show me favor in your unfailing love. Oh God, answer my prayer with your sure salvation. Pull me out of the mud, don't let me sink any deeper." That described my entire night.

The rest of the week, I took leaps and bounds in my faith that I never even expected to take. By the last night we weren't expecting anything more from God. But when we began to share what God had put on our hearts, soon everyone started confessing their deepest sins and asking for forgiveness and prayer. When our whole class gathered in a circle to pray for each other, I saw and learned true prayer.

Before the trip, I had believed in God but I didn't walk with Him. If I prayed, I would usually journal about a problem I was having that I wanted Him to fix. I saw God as compassionate and loving, but mostly as Someone who could be there to solve my problems.

All that changed in the DR. If I were to sum up what I learned, is was how to be bonded with brothers and sisters in Christ through prayer and worship, how to have a true day by day walk with my Savior, and how to make my time with Him be the highlight of the day. I thank God for that and I will remember it for the rest of my life.

Brittany Black, CVCA graduate:

I hadn't even planned on going on a summer CVCA trip. Eventually I signed up to go to Haiti, but learned about two weeks before leaving that we were all going to the Dominican. I was a little let down that our entire class would be together, because we were just separate cliques, each with their own friends. I was not really looking forward to it.

On the second night I wasn't feeling well, so I stayed back in my room and everyone else went upstairs for worship. Later they returned, crying and talking to each other, and I heard that they had "seen God" in the Upper Room. When I heard that, I wanted to cry myself because I'd missed it.

By the next night I was feeling a lot better and the Spirit was definitely present. As we were closing one of our songs, someone started crying out a prayer to God. Others started praying aloud and confessing things. It was an answer to my prayer that God would show himself to me. He showed up in that room, and I learned how to pray that night. I just talked to God and cried (although I'm not a very emotional person).

I also felt a connection with my classmates that came from His presence.

From then on, we felt the Spirit every time we had any sort of gathering. Even when we were out in the villages there was a new level of love and compassion for each other and for the Haitians. God shone through us the entire time.

Rick with Haitian boys in the Dominican Republic   *June 2006*

The week flew by. We were upset when it was time to go, but also glad because a spark had been ignited in each of our hearts and we were ready to share it with our families, churches and schools at home. Throughout the rest of the summer we met at different houses for worship. There might be seventy cars lining the street and one hundred of us in the house singing praises at ten o'clock at night. We didn't just let the fire die out after a few weeks; we kept it going.

Although our school was called Cuyahoga Valley Christian Academy, "Christian" hadn't formerly been a big part of a lot of the students' lives. Personally, my walk with God before the trip was on and off. I occasionally read my Bible or did devotions. I went to church every Sunday and youth group every Wednesday, and someone watching would say, "She has a pretty good walk with God." But I was living what Jim

would call a carnal Christian lifestyle and the DR completely opened my
eyes to what a real relationship is. It did that for a lot of us. Now we were
on fire to live up to our school name.

My relationship with God intensified so much within that one
week, just from getting up every morning and reading the devotionals.
Before, if you would have asked me to wake up at 5:30 a.m. for devotions,
I would have looked at you like you were crazy. But on the second day,
my friend, Shelby, and I set our alarms to get up early. The sun came up
as we were reading the devotion that Jim gave us, and it really sunk in that
we need to start our mornings with our Lord because without that we are
going down a different path than His. From that day on, I determined, "I
am going to start each day out right in my walk with God."

Since I came back from the DR I have been doing that. It's
amazing. When I am lazy and slack off, I notice a change in my day
and my attitude. All in all, my spiritual life was changed in ways that I
couldn't even imagine. I don't ever want to go back to how I was living
before.

Work on Elpidio's house   *June 2007*

Zack DiPaolo, CVCA graduate & trip leader:
   On the 2009 trip, I was looking forward to serving God through my ability to speak Spanish, as well as hopefully giving some guidance to the students.
   When the week started I was a little cynical, though. I knew that as a high school student I probably would not have bought into a lot of what was happening – but I'm glad those kids did. As the week went on, especially after Friday night when a lot of students began to break down and confess their struggles and sins, the cynicism left me. It was gone. Those kids were genuine and sincere in what they discovered in the DR.
   The trip also painted Christianity in a whole new way for me personally. I came away really excited about what I learned and eager to share it with others.

Linda Cowley, CVCA math teacher:
   I'd noticed that many of the kids who participated in MGM trips were genuinely changed. They were probably the biggest single reason that I finally went to the DR myself; I had to see what it was all about.
   In some ways, I found myself beginning the trip in the same spiritual condition as many of the students - certainly not on fire for the Lord, not using the power of the Holy Spirit in my daily life, and very lackadaisical in my own personal devotions. I came home having accepted the challenge to commit to thirty days of rising early, clearing my mind, spending time in prayer, and, most of all, spending time listening to God.
   I can't imagine the spiritual condition of our school if we hadn't offered the MGM trips for the past number of years.

Jerry Cowley, CVCA teacher and coach:
   On my first MGM trip I finally realized that to be spiritual means to be filled with the Holy Spirit (and I'd been a Christian for 35 years). I had an experience with God that led me to establish the life-changing practice of getting alone with God every day.
   On each subsequent trip something different happened that inspired me even further. Meeting God in Missions is a great place to do just that—meet the Lord while serving. Mr. McDonald's example has encouraged CVCA's leaders, teachers and coaches to model Christ in our lives.

Dale Schilling, CVCA teacher:
   I can remember when God first met me on December 26, 1986. Because I didn't stay grounded in the Word, I fell away and God let me fall pretty far. On the 2009 MGM trip to the DR, God brought me back.

I'd struggled just like the students did, and I identified with many things they shared. I think every CVCA teacher who is physically able ought to go on a Meeting God in Missions trip. I believe it's the one single thing that will put them in touch with the senior class and, more importantly, it will put them in touch with what God would do in their lives, and help cement what He's already done. It has done that for me.

Randy Tomich, CVCA Guidance Counselor:

On the 2009 trip I realized, above all, the need for connectedness between the CVCA students, faculty, and staff. Students need to trust us with their situations and problems so we can love them and help them. That needs to be our goal, and we will be praying and working on it.

We feel like as teachers and faculty we sometimes haven't been there for the kids, so we need to build bridges. And we need to start with the younger students in order to prevent some of the really hard things they will otherwise be going through. That is the bottom line. We know God has big things in store.

Dr. Don Lichi, Psychologist with Emerge Ministries and CVCA Board member:

Probably the best part of my MGM trips (I've been on three) are the morning devotionals with the emphasis Jim places on the changed heart. I've used them in numerous counseling sessions and also in a book that I am writing dealing with sexual purity.

The trips have also provided a wide variety of experiences. We've worshipped at the compound, interacted with Dominicans and Haitians, attended Dominican churches, visited sugar cane villages, and served in medical clinics. We've traveled up to the "mountaintop church" and visited the "cowboy church" and just been able to truly experience the Dominican culture. The trips have allowed the kids to get away for a period of time and be really challenged to grow in Christ. Jim has been very clear in his teaching, calling us all to be serious about our walk with the Lord and, particularly, to start having a devotional time. Through MGM, the Lord has powerfully impacted CVCA and my own life as well.

Marcia Lichi, CVCA Spanish teacher:

MGM has impacted the students of our school in two important ways.

First, these kids mostly come from upper-middle class families. Some are very wealthy. They have never seen how other people live or what it is like to be poor. It's so important they expand their view of the world and see what Jesus meant when He spoke of giving a cup of cold water in His name.

Second, the MGM trips have expanded their view of missions and highlighted the possibility of becoming a missionary. They see that it is not such a hard thing after all, that it is possible to go to another country, to get to know the people, and to work and live there.

I'm thankful for Jim and all of those who have been involved in providing a facility that allows us to experience God through missions.

Chrisi Kamp, CVCA teacher:

I was absolutely amazed by what the Holy Spirit did through our students on the 2008 trip. I'd never experienced anything like it. When I went home, I told my husband (who, like me, has also been on numerous mission trips) that he had to go to the DR - I couldn't even express to him in words what had happened. This year he went and I saw him just broken. He is a very quiet man, keeps many things to himself due to lots of hurt, and it was just amazing.

MGM combines missions with a spiritual camp for students and adults. No matter what the level of spiritual maturity, every person can grow. So while I believe we need to be involved with a variety of missions experiences at CVCA, I think an MGM trip needs to be the first trip any of our students go on because it's a life-changing experience.

David Kamp, CVCA Chemistry teacher:

The 2009 MGM trip was the first time in a very long time that someone sat me down and told me that I have got to surrender each day to the Holy Spirit in order to get beyond that day's trials and temptations. Someone reminded me how important it is combat Satan and yield myself to the Holy Spirit through morning devotions. The trip meant a rededication to God, a realization that I need to grow close to Him to feel complete in my inner being, and a fresh knowing that He is the only one Who supplies my needs.

Mark Meyer, Family Practice physician from Stow, Ohio:

The Meeting God in Missions organization is very appropriately named - when someone goes on those missions trips and allows God to work in their lives, they truly do meet Him. Many of the CVCA students, in particular, had been living their parents' faith until the DR experience forced them to make their faith their own as they were confronted with some very fundamental questions about Jesus, about God, and about what they believed.

The trips have also provided tremendous opportunities to witness upon returning to the U.S. Many patients ask me about the missions trips and even ask if they can send medications or make donations. Others ask how I can give up a week of vacation every summer to go to the DR. I tell them I don't know how I could not take a week of vacation to go there. Both my wife and I feel that those are the best weeks of our year.

Sue Meyer, physician:

Most medical missions trips involve just giving, giving, giving in the clinics - which I love to do. However, at MGM not only do I give, but I receive far more as Jim teaches what God has put on his heart and mentors those who are struggling. I've watched him take on the lives of confused teenagers, helping them see the reality of God, the importance of His love, and the power of the Holy Spirit to touch their lives, and also helping them make life-impacting decisions.

I feel like God made a way for CVCA to experience meeting God in missions. The kids gathered memories and stories and experiences that will be remembered for a lifetime, and they returned home changed. Although that's the desire of any ministry trip, MGM trips have a phenomenal track record for CVCA's students. God has allowed the DR to become a training ground - for our seniors, so they can step up and take on leading the school, and for our faculty, so they can become more effective for the students on a daily basis.

Rick Lyons, CVCA teacher, coach and trip leader (2006-2008):

The first year I was asked to lead our CVCA mission trip, it was in response to the trip the year before (our first year to MGM), and also a need to change our plans for Haiti. It was "Option B." That was all right, because I'd heard that wonderful things had happened when my local church had sent groups with MGM, and also when CVCA went the previous year, led by Jon Holley.

I had already been on two other trips with our junior classes which emphasized not only service, but also discipleship. For some, the discipleship component might seem unnecessary in a short-term missions setting. In reality, the impact that short-term missions has on a foreign community can be insignificant compared to the changes that can occur in a student's life - changes that play a significant role in their spiritual growth for many years and match our school's mission: "To educate and cultivate servants for Christ."

We were all more than pleasantly surprised with our MGM trip! The emphasis wasn't solely on serving for a limited time period. The emphasis was God—how did God show up today; what is God doing in this culture (when we went to evening church services); what is the Holy Spirit teaching you today? It became evident very early in the trip that our host, Jim McDonald, had not only a transformational encounter with God through a short-term mission trip himself, but was experiencing the transformational work of the Holy Spirit on an ongoing basis, because of the relationship he cultivates daily with his Heavenly Father.

God has redirected and transformed Jim's abilities and gifts as a coach into a communicator about God's game plan for the normal Christian. I say "normal Christian" because Jim has a Vince Lombardi style, but instead of "This is a football;" it's, "This is a Christian," "This is your heart," or "This is the Holy Spirit." He studies for a year to bring these distilled messages to the short-term missionaries that pass through MGM each week, and the concentration of his prayer, study and direction from God's Spirit is unmistakable. On more than one occasion, I've seen him coach a group to a simpler, more reasonable and effective faith.

Beyond that, he coaches groups and individuals to the point where each can "do business with God," because "the ball is now in their court." He does what many coaches hope to accomplish in an athlete's life: impart not only the means of success in the game, but the means of success in life—what it really takes. His transparency and obedience to the work of God's Spirit in his life has impacted hundreds of CVCA students and faculty in their seven to ten days with MGM in the DR.

In my personal life, I can point back to an encounter with God in the DR while Jim led a morning Bible study about the Holy Spirit and the heart. That meeting with God changed the way that I pray every morning. It also changed my outlook on the work of the Holy Spirit in my life on a daily basis.

In the life of our school community, I was again brought face to face with the work of the Holy Spirit on that 2008 trip. Our group was forever changed.

After three years of splitting our junior class, sending one to MGM in the Dominican Republic and one to Haiti, something had happened in Haiti which prompted a travel warning from the State Department. Because of this, I didn't feel comfortable sending a group of high school juniors there. At this time, I also was so impressed with what I'd already experienced while going to MGM each summer, and with what our students had gained from previous trips, that I started to see this as God's providence for our student body. Darla (my wife) and I both thought, "Wouldn't it be great if the whole class could experience God down at MGM, and not just half of the class?" I knew that there would be some opposition because of our strong, wonderful ties in Haiti, but I also knew that the whole class would be able to flourish on an MGM trip.

I immediately called Jim and asked him about the capacity of the MGM compound in Hato Mayor, because we'd need sleeping accommodations, food and water for about 130 people. Jim felt good about it, and it wasn't long before the logistics of such a trip were given a "thumbs up". When I met with our leaders and communicated the decision to our students, there were some downcast faces, to be sure. There was a lot of intellectual understanding and consent, but some of the adults who had invested in Haiti were not convinced of the benefits of going to MGM...until our trip.

CVCA Students in the Dominican Republic   *June 2008*

That 2008 trip has already been described by some of our students. It was early in the week, I believe the second night at the compound, when the adult leaders were meeting to decide on a course of action. One of our adults came in and said, "Do you know what's happening while we're meeting? Students are on their knees praying, crying and confessing sins." We all left our meeting quickly and observed God's great work.

No one had led them to this point except the willing hearts of our students and the Holy Spirit. And the Spirit continued to work the following night and through the week. God did what God wanted to do. You can't orchestrate a movement of God's Spirit, but you can come with open, willing, and passionate hearts for Him and then see what He wants to do. "Ask and it will be given to you; seek and you will find; knock and the door will be opened to you" (Matthew 7:7 NIV).

This was the Father's own "good gift" to His children. Praise the Lord! I had nothing to do with it; I could only observe, marvel, rejoice and enter in! His good work was thoroughly multiplied as each of these students, with transformed lives, entered their senior year, with faculty joining them in this wonderful community of discipleship – those looking to worship and be used daily by God.

These students, parents and faculty all agree that God has brought CVCA and MGM together and blessed our partnership in an unusual way. He has used it to accomplish His various purposes in many hearts and lives. And it appears that He intends to continue to bless us as we "share the road together" on this journey with Him.

Our partnership is one more chapter in the larger story, the story of this journey with God. It's a story that continues to be written. But what a blessing it has been for me to pause at this stage of the journey and look back, relive the beginning, retrace my steps, and rediscover God's hand in it all...

9

GOD'S AMAZING PURPOSE

Mary McDonald, granddaughter of Jim McDonald

My Journey With God

My amazing journey with God has brought me from the streets of Bridgeport, West Virginia, to the sugar cane villages of the Dominican Republic. And it's brought me from pain and frustration and anger to fulfillment and peace with God.

It was a long journey, not an overnight trip. Over the years, God worked through the disciplines of early quiet times with Him, weekly Sunday School lesson preparation, and the writing of MGM devotional booklets to completely change my perspective on myself, my marriage, my family, and church. And I look back with amazement at how often somebody would come up to me and say, "Here's a book that's pretty good. Maybe you ought to think about reading it." I can't tell you how many times people gave me material to read, or workbooks such as the Experiencing God by Henry Blackaby, that were just what I needed at the time.

Over the years a sort of pattern has emerged in my relationship with God: He takes me through periods of time where I'm content, and then all of a sudden He is introducing something new and I'm excited to be starting off on another leg of this journey with Him.

God and I have traveled together now for sixteen years, and I've begun to watch for what He is doing and rely upon Him to take me wherever he wants and provide for me whatever the occasion. He has opened up a wide range of opportunities for me to share what He's taught me, from churches to men's conferences to outdoor services. I am keenly aware, when I get up to speak, that I am a former basketball coach who understands basketball but who is totally dependent upon God to help me understand the Bible. As I've grown older my mind is not nearly as sharp as it used to be, yet it seems sharper than ever when it comes to remembering the Scriptures. When I'm discussing the Bible, God reminds me of things He has shown me before, bringing them back to my mind in His timing. Even so, while I'm closer to God than ever before, I am still on the learning curve and God is still on the teaching curve, and I anticipate that will be the situation until the day I go to heaven.

God has been also been faithful in bringing many people into my life who have enlightened me about the Word, helped me in writing devotionals, and helped me in Sunday School classes and in writing Sunday

Jenna at VBS in the Dominican Republic, CVCA Student   *June 2007*

School lessons. Only the power of the Holy Spirit working through these people and working on me has brought me and Meeting God in Missions to where we are today.

My role at MGM is changing. When I first started out in mission trips, I did labor work. Although I didn't have any skills, I could carry blocks and mortar and I could move boards around, as well as say a few words for morning devotions and evening church. Physically, I'm not able to do heavy duty labor anymore. I certainly could never do what I did in the beginning for even one day, working sunup to sundown, speaking at a church in the evening, getting to bed at nearly midnight, and then up the next morning to start all over again.

My contribution to Meeting God in Missions now focuses on preparing trips, getting people lined up for ministry responsibilities, going along to lead morning devotions, watching what goes on during the day, and maybe handling a problem or two along the way. Actually, I'm rather enjoying this role, and God has graciously continued to give me ideas and thoughts throughout the off-season so I can write the devotionals.

My wife and I have wondered hundreds of times, *How in the world did we get to this position with God, with the Dominican Republic and Haiti, with Meeting God in Missions, with people coming from all over the country and the groups grown to over one hundred on every trip? How did it evolve into this?*

Anyone with insight will realize my life journey has been driven by God from the very beginning. From my childhood He was preparing for the plan that He had for Meeting God in Missions, and He led every step of the way. He was there in the West Virginia days when I was wearing someone else's clothes and knocking on the door for food and unable to afford a doctor visit and moving from house to house. He was there when I thought I was going to make sports a livelihood and become a professional athlete. He was there to keep shutting the door on those plans because He had something better in mind.

As I look back on my life, I am absolutely convinced that He was continually preparing me for the time when I would become fifty-five years old and he would take me out of my comfort zone and I would begin this journey with God. I have never regretted this for a second. It has been the most exciting thing I could ever imagine.

I've often used the word "amazing" throughout this book. I'm amazed that God has been so abundantly faithful. I'm amazed by all the people who come on trips who I've never met or heard of before. I'm amazed at how involvement has spread by word-of-mouth. I'm amazed by money given to us out of the blue by people I will never see in this life.

Above all, I'm amazed that Mary Lou and I have found the purpose for which God created us. I believe it with all my heart.

And I also believe with all my heart that God has a purpose for everyone. Since the Garden of Eden through the present day, each person has been created in His image. Jeremiah 29:11-13 tells us that He has a plan for us and that we can only find the plan when we seek Him with all of our heart. Unfortunately, too few of us ever find that plan. But all who want to, can. I'm glad I did.

CONCLUSION

Has the journey been worth it? When I look back, I see myself at the pinnacle of my professional career. I am coaching at Edinboro and have been chosen as the National Coach for the United State Basketball Team. We've traveled to Israel for the competition, and won a gold medal. We are getting a team ready for the 1976 Olympics.

Then I see myself many years later standing in a sugar cane village, holding a little Haitian girl in my arms. The snot is running from her nose onto my shirt as she clasps her arms around me. I look down at her, and it dawns on me,

This is better than the gold medal I won in Israel. You can't get much better than this, holding this little girl out in the sugar cane fields.

God didn't create me for sports. He didn't create me for fame and glory. He didn't create me for making money and acquiring possessions. He hadn't planned any of those things for Mary Lou and I; He created us for a journey with Him. He planned for us to develop MGM, lead people to Christ, and have the opportunity to take people to a foreign country where they would meet God through missions. They'd have an experience with God there, and He would change their hearts until they would never be the same again.

Hundreds of those who have journeyed with God in Haiti and the DR have gone back home changed. They're serving God as never before in their family situation, in their local churches, and in their communities, and their lives will never be the same. They are finding their purpose in life. They are experiencing a journey with God.

You can, too. By asking Him to forgive your sins, which have already been paid for by Christ's death on the cross, and by turning every step of the rest of your life over to His leadership, you can join God on a journey that will take you safely from here to eternity...

... and what an amazing journey that will be!